Struggling for the Soul

THE POLITICS OF SCHOOLING AND THE CONSTRUCTION OF THE TEACHER

Struggling for the Soul

THE POLITICS OF SCHOOLING AND THE CONSTRUCTION OF THE TEACHER

THOMAS S. POPKEWITZ

Teachers College, Columbia University
New York and London

Published by Teachers College Press, 1234 Amsterdam Avenue, New York, NY
10027

Library of Congress Cataloging-in-Publication Data

Popkewitz, Thomas S.
    Struggling for the soul : the politics of schooling and the construction
of the teacher / Thomas S. Popkewitz.
        p.   cm.
    Includes bibliographical references (p.) and index
    ISBN 0-8077-3729-1 (cloth). — ISBN 0-8077-3728-3 (pbk.)
    1. Teach for America (Project)—Evaluation.   2. Teachers—Training
of—United States—Evaluation.   3. Socialization—United States.
4. Teaching—United States.   5. Education, Urban—United States.
6. Education, Rural—United States.   7. Educational equalization—
United States.   I. Title.
    LB1715.P58   1998
    371.1'00973—dc21   97-52181

ISBN 0-8077-3728-3 (paper)
ISBN 0-8077-3729-1 (cloth)

Printed on acid-free-paper

Manufactured in the United States of America

05   04   03   02   01   00   99   98   8   7   6   5   4   3   2   1

CONTENTS

ACKNOWLEDGMENTS

The data collection in this project was accomplished primarily with funds from Teach For America, with supplemental funds provided by the University of Wisconsin Graduate School. Different people were involved with the data at different times. Kathryn Densmore guided a group of observers during the Summer Institute. The work involved Cameron McCarthy, Carlos Torres, Marianne Bloch, Sigurjón Mydral, James Ladwig, and others. The data collection during the school year was accomplished with the help of Sigurjón Mydral, Wesley Martin, Julia Craddle, Monica Kirchweger, James Middleton, and Sheewa Cho. I also thank the corps members of Teach For America and its staff for the time provided during the year of collecting data. Sally Lesher served as project administrator and provided untold help in organizing the data files and writing a program for collating the data after a commercial system proved inefficient.

This book has taken 6 years to write, undergoing multiple drafts as its intellectual focus changed. As I wrote and rewrote this book, a number of people provided important intellectual comments. Lynn Fendler continually pushed my thinking about theoretical and methodological implications; Daniel Kallós gently helped me understand the difficulty of the story that I was writing in this study; and Dory Lightfoot continually challenged my thoughts and ways of expressing them. And there are others, such as Mimi Bloch, Dawnene Hammerberg, Catherine Cornbleth, Inés Dussel, Lizbeth Lundahl, Kim Wieczorek, Lew Zipin, the Wednesday Group at the University of Wisconsin, Ingrid Carlgren, Sverker Lindblad, the seminar group at the Pedagogical Institute, Umeå University, who provided important discussions as I tried to think about the ideas expressed. Sigbrit Frank-Wikberg, Geoff Whitty, and Allan Tom served as an advisory committee during the first year of the project. Michael Shapiro was always helpful in responding to my ideas and in suggesting literatures that give expressions to my initial thoughts. Dina Popkewitz is perhaps my best critic as she read through the drafts. I also thank Joann Foss, who helped me keep my sanity as I struggled in the final stages of finishing this manuscript. Her efficiency and kindness are deeply appreciated. Sarah Biondello of Teachers College Press has been all that one can ask for in an editor—

prodding me to tighten and clarify the texts. I appreciate as well her patience with me over the years. And finally, I want to specially thank Lea, who allowed me to disappear for days at a time when I was completing the book.

Thomas S. Popkewitz
Madison, Wisconsin
18 March, 1997

INTRODUCTION

In 1990, I was asked to evaluate Teach For America, an alternative teacher education program. It lies outside university certification programs and is designed to recruit and train people with degrees in fields other than education. The program focus was urban and rural schools where there are chronic shortages of teachers. The data collection for the research entailed "traditional" procedures associated with an ethnography—during the first year of the program, I observed and interviewed the staff and the program's recruits (corps members) as they worked full time in different schools around the country. From this initial fieldwork, it has taken me six years to write this study as I "played" with the interrelation of theoretical and empirical issues of the study of schooling.

The study began as one of socialization: What norms, patterns of practice, and systems of ideas construct the teacher in Teach For America? Underlying this question was a concern with issues of power and inequity: Teach For America was designed to provide teachers for schools that have consistently failed their children. How were the issues of miseducation being addressed, encountered, and countered?

My problem in the research was not to accept the classification of success or failure given in pedagogical discussions and policy statements of schools. These explanations of children's success and failure were not just neutral expressions to help the child learn and succeed. Neither was the problem, as so often stated in reform literature, merely to get teachers to feel positive that they and the children could be successful and to get rid of the labeling of children. It seemed to me that the languages of "helping" children embodied ways of reasoning about teaching and children and that the reasoning itself was the problem. That language of schooling, I thought, carried norms and values that historically function to intern and enclose children. What needs investigation, I thought, is not who succeeds or how success or failure is achieved but the systems of reasoning embodied in the ways we talk about success and failure.

But an uneasiness began as I struggled to think about the study of teacher education and schooling, an uneasiness related to my own thinking about the concept of socialization.[1] First, I realized that conventional notions of socialization of teachers did not tackle a persistent concern about how unequal education occurs. From the "hidden curriculum" studies begun in the 1970s to current discussions about neoliberalism, there has been a persistent concern with the issues of exclusion and inequalities related to schooling. These studies, it seems to me, have a continuity in that they point to how some groups use the resources of schools to their advantage while others do not, and that we still have an unequal society, which we need to challenge.

As I wrote the first drafts of this study, I felt I was reproducing the conventional "wisdom" about power that travels within the folklore of educational reform. My story would "tell" of the difficulties already known about urban and rural schools. The story would appear within the critical genre that raises questions about issues of schooling as a social and political enterprise.

Yet, as I wrote, I did not "see" anything in these first drafts to aid in understanding how the concrete pedagogical practices function to qualify/disqualify children in social affairs. Although I wanted to be sensitive to issues of race, gender, and class, my interest in knowledge as a political practice led me to think about the systems of reason as providing the principles of observation, supervision, and normalization that were somehow related to the questions of inequity in schooling. As Teach For America was a program for children of color and poverty, my suspicion was that the pedagogical ideas divided and differentiated children in the everyday practices of the teacher. Through identifying the dividing and differentiating strategies, I could better understand the disabling and disqualifying practices of teaching. Structural issues about the "state," economy, race, and gender, among others, were placed as a horizon, in a phenomenological sense, to the study as I focused on principles that ordered the reason and the reasonable person in teaching in urban and rural schools.

Second, my rethinking of the problem of power in schooling required a rethinking of the methods of ethnography. In one sense, this is an old argument: All research involves theoretical considerations as there are no data without theory. When we look at the classroom, we are involved in a process of selecting things to see and interpret. Our world is never one of tabula rasa but one organized through the principles of classification which are available to us to see and talk about our world. My focus on the "making" (constructing) of the teacher and the child shifted the analysis from previous concerns with what teachers mean when they talk about their work to the rules and standards by which that meaning is constructed.

This book, then, is about the pedagogical discourses that differentiate, distinguish, and divide the children and teachers who inhabited the urban and rural schools where Teach For America placed its recruits. But the argument of this book is that the pedagogical discourses are not unique to the schools of the program but are historically constructed discourses that give a specificity to the practices of *urban* and *rural* schooling. As I wrote the book, the story that I tell is less about the program, and more about the discourses of teaching, childhood, achievement, and school subjects that travel within education.

While there are important physical geographical distinctions, I will argue that the *urban* and *rural* child is discursively combined in the concrete practices of pedagogy. There were no distinctive pedagogical discourses to distinguish the urban from the rural teaching practices when talking about children's learning, achievements, or psychological characteristics. The same systems of pedagogical ideas circulated in the different geographical locations. For this reason, I use the two words as one—urban/rural. Further, my theoretical interest is to explore how the discursive practices produce the *urbanness/ruralness* of the child. This linguistic construction of urbanness/ruralness points to the manner in which the categories and distinctions of pedagogical practices assign *qualities* to the child. The urbanness/ruralness, I argue, constructs an oppositional space for the child—one whose qualities are different from others who are not explicitly mentioned in the discourses of teaching but are present through the classification of the urban and the rural school and child. This ethnography is about the classification of the *urbanness and ruralness of the child as a space in which the child can never be "of the average."*

CONSTRUCTING AN ETHNOGRAPHY: WHAT DO I MEAN BY POWER?

As I said earlier, after several decades of state educational planning and research to identify better approaches to classroom teaching—with the multitudes of "remediation" programs, community action projects, and state-funded research projects to identify "what works" and successful teaching—the uneven playing field of schools has continued almost uninterrupted, and the lives of children in schools are often worse now than when I started teaching in the 1960s. Large-scale state interventions and research closely tied to state programs to "rescue" children from the cycles of poverty and racism have not substantially changed the school. Sometimes, as I read critical educational literatures with a different rhetorical focus, I am at a similar loss. It seems almost as if the rhetorical and constant reiteration of the need to redress inequalities makes the problem confrontable and the ethical commitments reachable.[2]

My discomfort in contemporary educational debates made me think that possibly we have been asking the wrong questions. I thought about this in relation to my previous studies of schooling.[3] I realized that I had thought of power in a very particular way. Power was treated as "something" that was owned, a sovereign-owned power like in the days when kings ruled. Modern sovereignty belonged to bureaucracies of the schools, for example, which did not allow thoughtful teaching.

But this conclusion itself was based on certain assumptions about power that I now wanted to rethink, but not totally reject. The focus on sovereign power pointed to its ownership by professionals, the wealthy, the white, and so on. (The actual kings and queens in modernity no longer play a role in the construction of sovereign power; it is displaced to other social actors.) Modern ownership is not straightforward and unambiguous, but it is commonly believed that if power were properly identified, change could be promoted. Power, in this sense, should be confronted directly by identifying the practices that give some groups power and limit the access of others—community groups, parents. Access for those who were excluded from participation should be equalized by identifying and confronting the "owners" of power. Less directly, inclusion (access) is provided through school achievement and success for those who have previously not had success.

The reasoning of the sovereignty notion of power is, implicitly if not explicitly, like a mystery novel. If we can identify who perpetuated the inequities and how they dominate, then it is possible to change the distribution of power so that all groups can participate equally. The argument is a beguiling belief of 20th-century social theory and policy, particularly in post–World War II education. It underlies, as Hunter (1994) points out, the left and the right as they assume that the problem of schooling is a principled one: The difficulty is how to enable all groups to be included through the processes of schooling. It does not question how those principles are constructed as the effects of power.

This assumption of power shapes discussions of inclusion/exclusion in educational policy and research. Efforts are made to identify what "successful" teachers do in order to make their practices into universal practices for all teachers to follow. Discussions about empowerment and "voice" in education focus on the problem of how to include those people who have been previously marginalized and excluded.

These political projects of inclusion are important in a society that categorically has excluded different groups of people. But the focus on the categorical exclusion of groups does not answer the question about the systems of reasoning that organize the practices of "success," "empowerment," and "voice." That is, my interest is in the systems of reason that enable one to think of the "successful" classroom and the reasonable teacher in schools. My purpose is to examine systems of knowledge to understand how a particular urbanness and ruralness of the teacher and the child is produced to exclude and disable.

KNOWLEDGE AS THE EFFECTS OF POWER: MY POSTMODERN SENSIBILITY

This interest in the reasoning of schooling, however, did not come out of nowhere. Since the middle 1980s I have been reading literature that is now called postmodern social theory. While I use the term *postmodern*, I think of this theory not as anything "post" but as a broad band of literature that gave a historical specificity to the questions I had about schooling and inequality. The postmodern literature suggested to me that in thinking about schools, culture, and power, I had assumed more than I should in a critical stance toward schooling. The literature "told" me that I should pay more attention to the knowledge by which we reason about the "self" as teachers and researchers. That is, much of modern life is ordered through expert systems of knowledge that discipline how people participate and act. In a commonsense way, expert knowledge shapes and fashions "our" thinking and acting about the calories in our diet as contributing to our personal health; about the pollution in our environment as affecting our lives; about our body and mind as having stages of development, personality, and processes of self-realization; and about our children as having intelligence, growth, and a normal childhood. These thoughts that are assumed as natural are not natural thoughts; they are thoughts built from expert systems of knowledge. The power of such expert knowledge is that it is not only knowledge. Ideas function to shape and fashion how we participate as active, responsible individuals.

This fusion of public/personal knowledge that disciplines our choices and possibilities can be thought of as the effects of power. This notion of the effects of power is very different from that of sovereignty. I can say that it concerns the productive actions for our participation, where sovereignty focuses on what dominates and represses our actions.

Postmodern social theory became a political-social theory that I could use in the study of teaching. It directed me to understand that the very knowledge that organizes teaching, learning, classroom management, and curriculum inscribes a certain selectivity in what teachers "see," think, feel, and talk about regarding children and school subjects. The effects of that selectivity, I argue in this book, generate principles that disqualify many of the children from participation in the Teach For America schools.

This insight by itself is not original to postmodern literature, as critical research has continually alerted us to the relations of knowledge and

social divisions. But what the postmodern literature enabled me to do is
to provide more nuanced strategies to investigate pedagogical knowledge.[4]
As I stated earlier, the literature enabled me to rethink the idea of socialization by focusing on what we think of as true about teaching and children. It enabled me to think about why we want to know about children
in the ways that we do—why we talk about what is true, for example,
about teaching through psychological categories of childhood. It also enabled me to ask how teachers' reasoning about childhood relates to other
ideas, such as classroom management, "the wisdom of teachers' knowledge," and the schools of Teach For America as inner-city and rural.

The different discursive practices about teaching and children in school,
I argue in this study, are important social practices because they normalize children by placing them into a set of distinctions and differentiations
that function to divide the children into spaces. The spaces are discursive
rather than physical. The categories and distinctions construct boundaries
that "tell" us how to see the child as inhabiting a childhood, being a learner,
or achieving. Thus, with this theoretical "lens" I could investigate how
urbanness and ruralness represent a continuum of values about what is
normal and not normal. The discursive norms of average, normal, and not-
so-normal that I investigate in this study are not what is typically talked
about as teachers' beliefs or their philosophy of education. Neither are the
norms necessarily what is publicly spoken about as educational purposes.
Rather the norms are embodied in the categories, distinctions, differentiations, and divisions by which teachers come to "see" and act toward
children.

I see this book, then, not as a study of Teach For America per se, but
as an effort to understand how different discourses of pedagogy come together (I use the word "scaffolding") to generate principles for participation and action. For me, at this point, there is a system of reasoning that
historically circulates in schools about urbanness and ruralness, and that
reasoning is the "culprit" that needs to be investigated. I explore the divisions and distinctions embodied in this reason through the everyday,
commonsense activities and ideas about urban and rural schooling. In one
sense, this book did not start out as one about race in U.S. schools, but it
ended up as concerned with the production of distinctions and differences
that have implications for theories about racialization of the child.

With this aim, the book is written for reformers who propose to address issues of educational quality and inequities. This study is also written for teachers who seek to inquire critically into the systems of reasoning that organize their teaching. Making visible the rules through which
difference and diversity are normalized in teaching is a practical strategy
to open a potential space for alternative acts and alternative intentions that

are not articulated through available common sense. The theoretical and methodological foci of this study respond to issues of educational research concerned with the effects of schooling.

This book challenges certain notions about policy research, evaluation, and teaching. An assumption behind much contemporary discourse about teaching is that there are rational paths to salvation—the efficient school, the effective teacher, the authentic teacher. The world is seen as being based on certainty and on logically organized practices. Yet, when we look at the practices of policymaking and research, we find no moral, political, and cultural certitude. The promise of school research and evaluation lies not in foretelling what should be done to help "others," but in understanding the politics of knowledge that produce the subjects of reform. To say this somewhat differently, there is a strong reformist tendency in intellectual life that "says" that ideas are to be used in political projects. This study suggests that ideas inscribe political projects, and that a role of intellectual practices is to question the reigning dogma about intellectuals' signification of actors and the rules of progress.[5]

As I move into the analysis/interpretation, I recognize that I enter risky terrain that challenges prevailing research ideologies. My strategy of the study of educational reform is to scrutinize the knowledge of pedagogy. This approach destabilizes the available forms of reason that intern and enclose the spaces occupied by teachers and children, thus potentially opening those spaces for other possibilities. In this sense of moving against the grain, this book can be thought of as an act of resistance, but the resistance is different from that applied in theories of agency.

Once this is said, however, the analysis runs the risk of confronting the power of the imputed realities inscribed in the conventions of liberal and (certain) "left" scholarship. This imputed reality is one that "says" that when there is no identifiable sovereign power in the text, we must assume that there is no possibility of change or "agency." But my discussion does not forgo the recognition of a world that is socially constructed; neither does it eliminate reason as central to social change. If anything, my strategy is to destabilize reigning forms of reasoning through inquiring into how the objects of schooling are constructed—to understand how particular forms of knowledge inscribe power in ways that qualify and disqualify students from action and participation. To recognize how the categories, differentiations, and distinctions "set" agendas to guide action is to open up potential space for alternative practices that are silenced in the available common senses. The humanism I speak about is a reinsertion of our "selves" into history by understanding how the "self" has been humanly constructed through the material practices of knowledge itself.

Chapter 1

THE SPATIAL POLITICS OF URBAN AND RURAL EDUCATION

Constructing a Critical Ethnography

During the last decade, there has been a resurgence of interest in the problem of educational change. One of the most highly publicized of these reform programs is Teach For America (TFA).[1] In 1989, a senior at Princeton University proposed in her thesis that a private organization be created to find a solution to the shortage of teachers for urban and rural schools through an alternative teacher education program that would bring liberal arts graduates into teaching. After she graduated, funds were solicited from private businesses and foundations in order to develop an organization that would provide an alternative certification/teacher education program. By the end of the year following her graduation, the program was functioning with its first 500 recruits from the finest private and public universities in the nation. After an eight-week training session at the University of California, the students were placed as full-time teachers in rural Georgia and North Carolina; Baton Rouge and New Orleans, Louisiana; New York City; and the metropolitan areas of Los Angeles.

Teach For America held a great fascination for the American media, business, and philanthropic communities and for government, because the discourse concerning Teach For America claimed legitimacy within a wider American discourse about privatization and choice as a practice of policy.[2] TFA goals and justifications meshed with multiple streams of a general American social and political ideology in the 1980s. First of all, TFA drew on the idea that individual initiative and private enterprise can find solutions to the grave social issues of our time. Teach For America represented the utilitarian spirit of American enterprise, exhibiting a "can-do" attitude toward social problems. The program intended to change the way in which teachers were recruited and it attacked what was seen to be the entrenched ineptness of government bureaucracy. This last point was a legacy of

Reagan-era rhetoric about pulling government back from involvement in social affairs. The program also epitomized an idealism of youth that the country had not witnessed since the early days of the Kennedy era and the creation of the Peace Corps. Five hundred youths, most of whom had grown up with privilege, were committing themselves to spend two years working with people who were often denied any privilege. As if to evoke the image of the Peace Corps, TFA recruits were called "corps members."

This book is a report on an ethnographic study of Teach For America undertaken during its first year of operation.[3] Its observations, interviews, and surveys were conducted as the corps members worked in classrooms and participated in training sessions that were to prepare them as teachers. This book, however, uses the ethnography data in a special way. It takes the categories Teach For America utilized as a program to improve the teaching and teacher education of urban and rural schools and interrogates those ideas. Drawing on postmodern social and feminist theories, it gives attention to how discourses of urbanness and ruralness are part of an amalgamation or scaffolding of discourses about teaching, learning, and managing the child. The scaffolding of ideas, I argue, forms a grid to give intelligibility through the categories, differentiations, and distinctions that normalize the urbanness and ruralness of the child in the schools. I use the idea of *urbanness* and *ruralness* to consider how various discourses of teaching, learning, and childhood are scaffolded. This scaffolding or overlapping of different discourses of teaching functions to construct the qualities and capabilities of the child who inhabits the schools. This approach to research suggests that there is no child, as an object-of-study, in a school until discursive strategies are applied to enable one to "see," think, talk, and feel about the object of study in school. In this sense, the *urbanness* and a *ruralness* of the school and the child is "made" through the scaffolding of discourses about the child, teaching, and learning. Thus, to approach the assumptions about urban and rural schools, research cannot regard them as geographical concepts; they are discursive concepts that historically circulate in schooling to construct the qualities and capabilities of the urban and rural child.

Further, that history involves the merging of the rural and the urban in particular institutional settings. In the 19th century, pastoral images of the countryside were related to those of industrialization. The new national imaginary was about citizenry and community that combined a rural notion of aesthetics and purity with cosmopolitan wisdom and rationality (Marx, 1964; Sennett, 1994). This national imaginary, however, changed in the late 20th century, particularly as State welfare discourses about poverty targeted specific groups in need of administration. Educational discourses (as well as those of other "poverty" discourses) constructed

a space of *urbanness* and *ruralness* that was different from and in opposition to the space that previously formed the cosmopolitan and pastoral
images (Hennon, in press). I use the notion of space to talk about "urban"
and "rural" because there are no distinctions among the two phrases when
examining the concrete discourses of pedagogy in this study. The discourses
of teachers applied the same concepts of school subjects, learning, achievement, and teaching whether they were in a rural or urban school. In effect, the urban and rural children were united by a subjectivity that was
distinguishable from the subjectivities of "others" who are not spoken about
in the discourses of teaching. But the qualities of "being" urban and rural
(the *urbanness and ruralness of the child*) constructed a place that lies outside of reason and the standards of the normal.

To recognize the construction of this new and oppositional space of
the "urban" and "rural," one might ask about the very comparison that is
being made. Urban and rural as compared to or in opposition to what?
Yet the focus on the phrase "urban" provokes no clear opposition. Yet once
spoken, everyone "knows" what is being talked about. One has to stretch
the imagination to compare the urban, for example, to the "suburban."
But that does not stand in a symmetrical opposition to the qualities signified by the term "urban." For example, there are "urban" schools in suburbia as found outside of Los Angeles or on Long Island. The urban, then,
does not signify a geographical place but it gives reference to certain unspoken qualities of the child and community who belongs in that space.
The same applies to the phrase "rural." As the professional and business
community moves out to the farmlands outside of Madison, for example,
those areas are no longer "rural" but now called "suburbia" even though
the areas are populated mostly with cows and corn fields.

What is interesting about the classifications, then, is its being embedded in a discourse that functions to normalize the qualities of people who
are perceived as different. Urban and rural education are words that are
historically linked to specific systems of reasoning that differentiate and
divide the "urban" and "rural" child and teacher from others. The categories are the effects of power. The "others," outside of the space of the urban
and rural, need no categories or distinctions to tell of their presence. But
the norms of those who are absent in the discourses of urban/rural education silently pervade the systems of classification.

It is in this theoretical sense of discourse and power that the significance of Teach For America is understood in this ethnography. My concern is not with its program but with the pedagogical discourses that
circulated within its various activities. Teach For America, then, is not important for its recruitment practices or with the ways in which teachers
are prepared for urban and rural schools. Rather its significance is as an

exemplar to consider how the concrete discourses of American urban and rural schools constructed systems of distinctions and representations that qualify and disqualify children from participation and action.

This first chapter provides both a brief description of Teach For America during its first year, and the theoretical "setting" by which I approached the data analyzed. I pay particular attention to the relation of knowledge and power that forms the intellectual horizon by which the ethnography was constructed. I wanted to call this book *The Spatial Politics of Educational Knowledge: Constituting the Urban and Rural Teacher* to call attention to how the discourses about teaching and learning produce an imaginary "room" or space from which the child is "seen," talked about, and acted on. The "spatial politics" is related to how the discursive practices of pedagogy enclose and intern the child as "different" and outside of the normal. The differences, however, are not imaginary; they are productive in the sense of functioning to disqualify the children from participation and action.

My focus on spatial politics recognizes that schooling produces multiple social spaces and this study concerns the particular discourses deployed within urban and rural schooling. In a study of a national program for reforming elementary schools, for example, different systems of knowledge were identified to give direction and purpose to the organization of classrooms (Popkewitz, Tabachnick, & Wehlage, 1982). The different pedagogical practices were related not only to internal dynamics of the school but to the social/cultural and political context of the community in which the pedagogical knowledge was realized. Further, the distinctions of urban and rural, when deployed in a scaffolding of discourses, can refer to systems of inclusion rather than to exclusion. When thinking of urban, for example, one can focus on what is urbane, cosmopolitan, and sophisticated. Historically, the notion of rural, as well, can capture the norms of participation in a liberal democracy, relating political norms to the pastoral images of trust and security associated with small town communities. This study's focus on the scaffolding of discourses historically deployed within urban and rural schooling is to explore how these discourses produce a single, particular political space that historically targets ethnic, racial, and minority groups.

Further, my concern with the urbanness and ruralness of schooling is to recognize their fluidity and contingency. In most European and Latin American nations, for example, the city is an enclave of wealth. There, different systems of categories and distinctions are deployed to target the poor and minorities, who live outside the city (but often are rural). This study, then, can be read as *both* providing a detailed analysis of the discourses mobilized to produce systems of exclusion in the United States *and* as a method to study the spatial politics of educational knowledge through its focus on the scaffolding of discourses. The actual conceptual distinctions and discursive relations in different historical contexts require a historical specificity to the strategy of governing deployed.

My concern with discourses as systems of knowledge, then, is not only with the structures within which concepts and explanations are formed. My use of discourses is to direct attention to the intersection of multiple knowledges that govern the practices of teachers. Further, it is to consider how the knowledge systems of pedagogy function in constructing the space that is called urban and rural schooling—particularly as a space whose images function to qualify or disqualify children from action and participation.

My argument is that the systems of everyday reasoning of schooling are the loci in the battle for more equitable schooling and a more just society. Yet, in engaging in this battle, teacher educators, teachers, and administrators have precious little understanding of how concrete systems of ideas embodied in classroom practice work to produce the unequal playing field that we call schooling. While not providing answers to questions about what alternatives to seek, I intend to disrupt the way we "tell the truth" about ourselves as teachers and children and thus open a potential space for alternatives.

TEACH FOR AMERICA AND PRIVILEGING
SCHOOL PRACTICES

Teach For America made the transition from being a "good idea" to being a national organization in a remarkably short time. From the beginning of 1990 to the summer of that year, it had constructed the Summer Institute and recruited 500 corps members.

Teach For America sought legitimacy by focusing on two constituencies—business and school districts. The goal of the national office was to organize its image to appear corporate while also dealing directly with teachers, school districts, and corps members. At the same time, Teach For America sought to build its legitimacy apart from the influence of existing agencies that carried on certification processes—that is, schools of education.

The position of Teach For America in relation to school districts and an "on-the-job" training system has a certain irony. It is ironic because it positioned Teach For America as a source of recruitment and training of teachers for urban and rural schools with high rates of failure. As I will argue in later chapters, Teach For America's relations with schools and state departments of public instruction included more than a working, collaborative arrangement. Embodied in the working relations were the discursive practices of schooling through which children of color were classified for instruction. Thus, while Teach For America sought to distance itself from the institutional organization of teacher education, it did not distance itself from or scrutinize the discursive practices that linked teacher education and schools.

Organizing for Teaching: The Summer Institute and Los Angeles Schools

The 8-week Summer Institute held at the University of Southern California (USC) symbolically reflected the image of Teach For America. The juxtaposition of the university with its immediate surroundings projects the three tenets of Teach For America: the affluence of America's privileged, the commitment to those who have been denied privilege, and the need to address social and cultural diversity. Staff, faculty, and corps members lived on USC's campus during the training.

The recruitment of corps members was modeled on the Peace Corps—active recruitment, short time commitment, selective and centralized application process, intensive training, placement, and a support mechanism.[4] The institute was an intensive 15-hours-a-day, 6-days-a-week, 8-week training program to prepare the recruits with teaching skills and cross-cultural understanding and to provide them with intensive experience in schools as student teachers. The stated goal of the institute was:

> to prepare the Corps Members to be thinking teachers who aren't tied to one educational strategy or model but who approach each situation as decision makers. We aim to prepare them specifically to be effective in the particular environments in which they will be placed, so there will be a heavy emphasis on education that is multicultural. (Teach For America, n.d., p. 8)

Another goal of the Summer Institute was to make the teacher an agent of change. Drawing on a curriculum tradition of social reconstruction that emerged during the 1930s, the institute sought to focus on contemporary issues of social inclusion in a demographically and economically changing United States.

The first 2 weeks were comprised of foundational lectures (sociology, psychology, history of education) as well as an introduction to multicultural education. Further, corps members were organized into "learning communities" that discussed methods of teaching and issues across the curriculum. Multicultural curriculum was emphasized to focus on TFA's concern for urban and rural schooling; environments that have a large proportion of people of color and a high incidence of poverty; and schools

that have high teacher turnover, inadequate staffing, and a high proportion of academic failures.

Each corps member was then placed in a Los Angeles Unified School
District (LAUSD) classroom to work with an experienced cooperating
teacher for 6 weeks. There they spent the mornings in the classrooms; the
afternoons were assigned, in most instances, to teacher education classes
that corresponded with the subject area they would teach in the fall.

The positioning of the corps members in Los Angeles introduced a
complex social dynamic into the web of learning about teaching. The placement of the institute on the USC campus symbolically related the public
image of TFA to its meliorative vision—juxtaposing a private, prestigious
university with a surrounding urban blight that typifies cities in the United
States. The relatively high percentage of people of color within the corps
(29%) further mixed the images, agendas, and social consciousness as
teaching was discussed during the eight weeks.

Organizing for Urban and Rural Schools

Among the schools where Teach For America placed its corps members,
the two rural districts in Georgia and North Carolina were in counties that
were home to both blacks and whites, with the county school systems
having a greater percentage of blacks. This racial imbalance in the schools,
according to one school superintendent, is the product of a private acad-
emy system that siphons off the wealthier white students. Of the students
who do go to the public schools, most do not go on to higher education,
and as one principal stated, "those who [do] go are talented, move away,
and don't come back." There is also a higher rate of poor school achievement and a higher dropout rate among blacks than among whites.

Administrators highlighted community isolation, limited opportuni-
ties for social interaction and recreation, and low teacher morale as restrict-
ing the districts' ability to attract qualified teachers. In one of the districts,
the superintendent predicted that within 5 years there could be as much
as a 50% turnover rate among teaching staff.

The urban districts posed no fewer difficulties for Teach For America
to address. Poverty in the city, shortages of adequate instructional resources, threats of teacher layoffs in New York City, and lack of knowledge about bureaucratic procedures were constant sources of anxiety
among corps members. Moreover, most of the schools visited had a high
percentage of children from low-income families who also scored well
below standard on achievement tests.

Within this context, we can understand Teach For America as responding to a strong staffing problem of U.S. schools. In particular, the corps

members who taught science, mathematics, and foreign languages provided instruction in areas that administrators cited as being resistant to recruitment.

The urban schools posed different logistical problems than the rural schools. Although the diversity among these districts is striking, corps members were generally placed in schools located in densely populated areas, and the districts we visited in this study were characterized by low-income populations and high rates of attrition among both teachers and students.

Classes were not only crowded, they were often challenging in physical terms. Two beginning teachers discovered that their urban school compelled them to take down all of their classroom displays and bulletin boards as they were moved to other classrooms—to accommodate the rotating, year-round school schedule. These "roamers" and their pupils simply did not have a room of their own. In some places there were no funds for supplies; in others the supply budget was limited—sometimes as little as $30 a year. In comparative terms, however, it is clear that the material resources that were available to corps members varied both within and across districts and regions. Where new textbooks were not available, older ones, some from the early 1980s, were brought into service.

CONSTRUCTING A CRITICAL ETHNOGRAPHY

Once the above description of Teach For America is offered, it still leaves the theoretical question of how to organize a critical ethnography concerned with issues of power. The notion of theory that I use here is one of "lenses" or linguistic framing that exists prior to, but is modified during and after, data collection. Theory, in the sense that I use it, "tells" us what "things" are to be seen and interpreted from the infinite number of events and action of schooling. Theory, then, is a process through which things are sorted, related, and omitted from thought. My thinking about "theory," then, is not as a deductive set of propositions to test (a positivist notion of knowledge), but rather as a set of epistemological distinctions to orient the observer toward the empirical world, but whose actual concepts and descriptions involve a continual interplay between the theory and events of the world. For example, the specific categories and relations that organize this study emerged through a complex process of data analysis and "playing" with conceptual "tools" that could give intellectual focus to those empirical data.[5]

Part of the theory that organized this ethnography is to view Teach For America as an exemplar of educational reform and schooling rather than to view the program as the case itself. While most research takes for granted the idea of a case study as the specific context in which data are collected, the idea of a case is itself a complex theoretical problem that requires a self-reflectivity rather than acceptance of a particular chronological event, for example, as the boundary of the case (see Appendix). Thus, the initial task of the study is to consider how to think about what this program was a case of: Was it a case of recruitment, of the privatization of social policy, or, as I eventually decided, of the productive power of educational discourses?

A number of different issues were brought into a conversation about how this program should be thought about and studied. One was directing attention to the difficulties of education in urban and rural schooling. Implicit in this labeling is the realization that the context of schooling is an unequal playing field. In some ways, the study of Teach For America would have to direct attention to schooling in an unequal society.

Reflecting on previous research about inequalities, I thought that possibly we have been asking the wrong questions. My previous studies of schooling sought to understand the "culture" of the classroom that conceptualized power as a problem of sovereignty. Put simply, the concept of sovereign power directs attention to "something" owned by teachers and/or students, and the fact that that ownership can be redistributed among groups in social arenas, hence the use of the term *sovereignty*. The sovereignty view of power is found in the notion of democratic schools, which asks who participates (and is given "voice") and who is excluded from the decision making of schooling. Previously, I used the sovereignty concept of power to understand how different groups' interests repressed others, focusing on, sometimes directly and sometimes indirectly, bureaucracy, gender, race, and social differentiations as denying an equitable schooling (see, e.g., Popkewitz, 1976; Popkewitz et al., 1982).

However, as I said in the Introduction, I was uneasy with this interpretation. I felt that my narrative was repeating theoretically what I and others have said consistently since the 1970s—schools work in inequitable ways and differences exist. The "hidden curriculum" literature forcefully directed attention to the social, political, and economic effects of pedagogical practices (see, e.g., Young, 1971, as an icon of this period). As I compared those studies with today's literature, the major differences between then and now seemed to lie in the policies rather than in substantive development of the issue of power. Today's talk about neoliberal theories and conservative restorations points to different policy languages and "contexts" than those of the 1970s, but the conclusions are the same—some groups use the resources of schools to their advantage while others do not, with little focus on the concrete practices that produce an unequal society.

My uneasiness was given further focus by my reading of recent social science and feminist scholarship that is often called "postmodern." The literature suggests that although liberal, conservative, and left scholarship have different ideological positions, they maintain similar images of the sovereign actors who act and participate.[6] Judith Butler (1992), for example, suggests that the sovereign model of power uncritically takes the locus of the struggle for knowledge as being about enfranchisement and democracy. This uncritical acceptance of actors who repress/are repressed, she argues, often consolidates and conceals power relations even while attempting to "restructure" them. Thus, while the sovereignty notion of power is important in giving representation to groups previously marginalized, it has not directed attention to how the knowledge of teaching inscribes prior systems of classification that function to disable, disqualify, and marginalize children (see Popkewitz & Brennan, 1998).

This chapter, then, is about my journey to understand the politics of knowledge embedded in the pedagogical practices of Teach For America. My concern inverts Marx's concern with the productive characteristics of labor into a concern with the productive characteristics of knowledge itself (Dumm, 1987).

The study departs, then, from ethnographic studies by the way in which it conceptualizes power. Rather than focus on power as a question of who rules (or who is ruled—the sovereignty concept of power), my concern is with how the different pedagogical knowledges "make" (construct) the teacher who administers the child. I argue that knowledge of pedagogy is a constitutive, material element of the contemporary world. Not only do the rules of "reasoning" about teaching and childhood "tell us" what to notice (and not to notice), what things belong together, and what things are not "thinkable" within the rules and standards of the thinking applied; the knowledge systems of teaching also embody a continuum of values whose consequence is to compare children discursively through the distinctions, norms, and divisions linguistically produced in pedagogy. The constructions of pedagogical discourses normalize in a way that functions to disqualify certain children from participation, but this disqualification occurs through the norms that place the child's capabilities and "being" in a space that lies outside of reason itself. This study, then, is a deliberate strategy to displace conventional ethnographies that take for granted the position of the actor, the knowledge of pedagogy, and the "naturalness" of the speech. In its place is a study of power as the effects of the systems of knowledge through which reason is formed and the objects of reflection are constructed.

POWER AS PRODUCTIVE: SOME CONCEPTUAL DISTINCTIONS IN THE STUDY OF URBAN AND RURAL EDUCATION

In a general sense, this study is about the socialization of teachers. But it is not concerned with the actions of teachers in schools per se, or with how their participation produces beliefs and norms. The interest of this study is how the realities are constituted for teachers to act and make teachers' existence seem practical. My starting point is to consider urban and rural education as discursive practices that historically deploy particular systems of thought and rules of reason. These rules and systems produce limits and boundaries to what is possible and not possible for the teacher who works with children. While the concepts of *urban* and *rural* are analytically distinct, the separation of the words does not hold up empirically. The *urbanness* and the *ruralness* of the child and the teacher are constructed through similar and overlapping pedagogical discourses.

This study, then, challenges two different distinctions of contemporary education. One is the distinction between urban and rural education. Discursively, there is no practical distinction when the concrete pedagogical practices that order and divide children and teachers are examined. To underscore this relation, I use the single word "urban/rural" to indicate the ways in which the two concepts are mutually related. For literary reasons I also conjoin the terms: urban and rural.

Second, I have sought to reverse the ways in which the concept of socialization has been used. Where traditional notions of socialization are viewed as controlling and repressing, my interest is in the discourses of schooling as disciplining and producing action. The study, then, reverses the traditional notion of power as repression to think about how power operates as a productive element in social life—how the knowledge of pedagogy "makes" the teacher and the child who is qualified or disqualified from participation.

A simple way of initiating a conversation about this productive notion of power is to think of what happens when one goes to a supermarket. The "educated" shopper has all sorts of "rules" and distinctions about acceptable foods. One central set of organizing principles is in the labeling, such as the categories provided about fat content, calories, sodium, and so on.

But this food labeling is not only an ordering table about the content of food. The statistical percents of the "content" and the ordering of ingredients produce a way of "telling the truth" or the reason by which one thinks about and acts as a healthy, desirable, sometimes "sexual," and "reasonable person." That "telling of truth" embodies multiple sets of calculations or rationalities. The food labeling connects political rationalities about a healthy society and citizenry, medical discourses about growth and disease, commercial interests in food production, scientific discourses about diet, and gendered discourses that embody images of sexuality (differentiated images of the "trim" and "fit" body). The presentation of the "health" of foods involves a grid of selections that is also a set of omissions, such as the nondistinctions about the genetic engineering of the food, the pesticides and hormones used, and so on.

The simple classification systems on boxes of food, then, are not simple but are bound into a grid that gives intelligibility and the "will to know." The labeling embodies a system of reason that is productive of how we think, see, act, and talk about the actions related to our "self"—governing through the discursive practices what is desirable, healthy, and personally satisfying.

This governing of the self is also a function of pedagogy. The development of the 20th-century school connected the scope and aspirations of public powers with the personal and subjective capacities of individuals. Education tied the new social welfare goals of the state with a particular form of scientific expertise that organized subjectivities—the principles generated to organize the thinking, feeling, hoping, and "knowing" capacities of the productive citizen. Teaching and learning (the two are tied together) produce a self-governed individuality. The effects of the knowledge deployed in curriculum "make" the rules for defining and solving one's personal problems.

The productive quality of power in pedagogical practices can be pursued through four distinctions about knowledge that underlie the analysis and interpretation of this study. These distinctions direct attention to the discourses of teaching as a practice of normalization, the functioning of educational psychology as a pastoral power, the spatial politics of urbanness and ruralness, and, finally, an alchemy of schooling in which the child and school subjects are denuded of social mooring. The productive concept of power does not eliminate questions about how outside social interests and forces (i.e., the sovereignty concept of power) dominate in schooling, but gives prime attention to the "thought" and reason of schooling as producing divisions that generate an unequal playing field.

Normalization of the Child

We can think of norms as an integral part of ideas about children's development, achievement, and the interactions of teachers and children (see, e.g., ethnographic studies of classrooms in Graue, 1993; McNeil, 1986; Page, 1991). My concern with normalization, however, in this study is not those norms that give value and legitimacy to school processes. The normalization that I speak about directs attention to how linguistic practices function to separate and compare children along a continuum of values.

If we think about simple conversations that occur in school, we recognize language as constructing norms that are different from those of institutions or personal expressions. It is not uncommon, for example, for a teacher to make distinctions about learning. There are distinctions about how children master content (grade-level distinctions, basal reader distinctions, and so on) that embody norms about stages of growth and achievement.

There are other distinctions that are less obvious but also embody a normalization of the child. In this study, the distinctions between a child's intelligence and his or her potential seem to address a child's "natural" ability and the teacher's desire to provide successful learning environments. The idea of intelligence seems to stand as a universal value from which this judgment about intelligence is applied to the specific child.

Yet, the use of the words *intelligence* and *potential* is embedded in a set of pedogogical distinctions and differentiations that locates the child along a continuum of values. The talk about children's intelligence, as I argue in Chapter 2, is visioned within a distinction that a particular child has "street-wise intelligence." The distinction "says" that there is something that is intelligence, but the child's street-wise intelligence is different. Here, the distinctions and divisions of intelligence inscribe a normalization of the child as having qualities of being that are different from those of others. The distinction is visioned in the discourse rather than as overt and categorical (such as making sure that as many girls as boys take mathematics courses).

This normalization is different from labeling theories that are most often used when talking about the languages of schooling. Labeling theories focus on the categorical imperatives of words, that is, certain words are used to define the identities of children as they travel through schools. These words are viewed as defining the expectations and demands made on children and their "self-fulfilling" prophecy in determining success and failure. My concern with the systems of reasoning gives focus to something different. It is not a concern with the "labels" applied but with the systems of "reason" produced that define what is inside or outside the norms of competence, achievement, and salvation.

The norms that distiguish the intelligence of the child are part of a grid of ideas through which the teacher differentiates and divides. The grid of ideas about learning, childhood, teaching, and curriculum function objectively to separate and rank individuals by creating finer and finer differentiations of everyday behavior (Dreyfus & Rabinow, 1983).

This leads us to a second point about normalization. The ranking and dividing does not occur on an equal playing field. Discursive patterns generate principles that include and exclude individuals for participation and action. The norms embedded in intelligence, learning, and the "self-esteem" of the child (frequently used terms in pedagogy) function to disqualify certain children who do not "fit" the norms of the average.

The functioning of pedagogy as a system of inclusion/exclusion can be considered more closely through a taken-for-granted assumption of educational discourses of reform. That assumption, found in Teach For America, is that there is a need for recruitment and training programs for teachers in *urban* and *rural* schools.[7] The words are ostensibly placed in school reform to signify a humanitarian effort to provide resources to schools that have consistently failed in their social and ethical purposes.

But the words *urban* and *rural*, I have argued, embody distinctions and divisions that signify something that is qualitatively different from the intended humanitarian purposes. The words embody a coding in American schooling that separates certain schools (and children) from other schools. These "other" schools and children are not named in the distinctions that order teaching but are silently present. This silent presence occurs through a dual quality of the normalizations. The pedagogical discourses inscribe the norms that exist as the average. There is the average or normal state of affairs according to which all children are to be understood and evaluated, even those who are urban and rural. Present in the discourses are also the norms of the future from which progress and amelioration can be obtained. The norms of the pedagogical practices produce a composite figure of perfection toward which the children may progress. In this combining of averages and progress, the discourses of urban and rural education link the "is" and the "ought" (for a discussion of this aspect of normalization, see Hacking, 1990).

The linking of the norms to progress in the discourses of urban and rural tie the Teach For America program with other discourses of social and educational policy in the contemporary American landscape. Historically, the focus on urban and rural schools is part of a longer trajectory of school reform, capturing a 19th-century view of schooling as a means to "rescue" children from their economic, social, and cultural conditions through planned intervention. The notion of rescue combined religious views of salvation with secular notions about the effects of poverty, class, and social/racial discrimination. Historically, the groups to be rescued by schools, however, are not merely those who were marginalized, but also the middle classes who sent their children to school.

But to place children in spaces of urban and rural schools signifies particular populations to be administered and rescued. The particular systems of ideas differentiate and divide the child as different from some other child who is silently present but not spoken about. That different urban (sometimes inner-city) and rural child is present in discourses of psychological development and learning (such as learning styles), conceptions of school subjects taught (such as children learning content through "hands-on" experiences), distinctions about children's intelligence, and technologies of classroom management. The urbanness and ruralness of the child are also related to state welfare policies that target certain populations who are in need of remediation and that join discourses about the psychological and cognitive effects of being "inner-city" and "rural." The different sets of ideas form a grid that orders how the children of the school are thought of and acted on as learners/nonlearners, and the competence of the teachers who perform in classrooms.

Again, I must emphasize that the construction of urbanness/ruralness has less to do with the geographical location of a school than with the qualities of "being" ascribed to children and teachers. Anyone familiar with the American landscape would immediately recognize, for example, that *urbanness* is a quality that is equally applied to suburban schools where there are large populations of poor and people of color, but does not apply to children who live in the expensive or professional areas of the city, neither is "rural" applied to the new developments of the countryside.

What is important in this study, then, is to consider the classification of urban and rural as embodying systems of ideas that govern and discipline actions. The governing is not of a principal who says that a teacher needs to give a test every week, or of a department of education that mandates the teaching of local history in third grade. These are negative notions of power that prevent action. The governing that I speak about is positive and productive through providing principles of reasoning for actions and reflection about teaching. Governing is not only what is cognitively understood, but the production of norms that separate and divide according to the available sensitivities, dispositions, and awarenesses. The principles of reasoning discriminate, distinguish, and normalize what the child is and is to become.

Pedagogy, then, can be understood as the effect of power through its processes of normalization. Two elements of that normalization are explored here. One is the discourse of educational psychology, particularly as it functions pastorally to open up the dispositions and sensitivities of the child to supervision and correction. A second element is a populational reasoning in pedagogy. This involves the division and administration of children through an individualization that "makes" particular attributes of a group the essential characteristics of the person.

Pastoral Power: Power, Redemption, and Rescuing the Soul

A commonplace in contemporary schooling is to think about teaching as a problem of psychology. Most curriculum discussions focus on psychological ideas about how children internalize information (learning, cognition), and ideas about the self-worth and development of the child (such as self-esteem as a prerequisite for learning). In fact, it is almost impossible to talk about schooling in today's world without the deployment of psychological categories.

But this deployment of psychology is not a neutral or a natural act; it is the product of history, and a technology of power and normalization. I introduce the term *technology* to talk about psychology in order to recognize how different ideas and practices combine to produce means that govern, shape, and fashion the conduct of individuals. My discussion of psychology as a technology goes against the grain as we think of technology as associated with the natural and physical world, not the social world. But we can also think that

> our very experience of ourselves as certain sorts of persons—creatures of freedom, of liberty, of personal powers, of self-realization—is the outcome of a range of human technologies, technologies that take modes of being human as their object. Technology, here, refers to any assembly structured by a practical rationality governed by more or less conscious goals. Human technologies are hybrid assemblages of knowledges, instruments, persons, systems of judgments, buildings and spaces, underpinned at the programmatic level by certain presuppositions and objectives about human beings. (Rose, 1996b, p. 26)

This notion of psychology as a social technology enables us to recognize that the invention of a modern scientific psychology reverses an important hierarchy of power that dominated until the 19th century. In feudal and monarchical systems, individualization was greatest at the summit of society. Power was visibly embodied in the top of the social political hierarchy—the king and his court. The new patterns of governing in the 19th century, in contrast, focused power on persons in everyday life. Social policy and expert knowledge focused on the regulation of individual self-reflection, self-examination, and consciousness.

The individualization worked through an inscription of the religious confessional that joined the public and private. Power worked through discourses of individualization that made the soul the subject of observation, scrutiny, and self-examination and self-confession.

> The conviction that truth can be discovered through the self-examination of consciousness and the confession of one's thoughts and acts now appears so natural, so compelling, indeed so self-evident, that it seems unreasonable to posit that such self-examination is a central component in a strategy of power. This unseemingness rests on an attachment to the repressive hypothesis; if the truth is inherently opposed to power, then its uncovering would surely lead us on the path to liberation. (Foucault, quoted in Dreyfus & Rabinow, 1983, p. 175)

The effect of pastoral power decentralized the individual by making specific attributes and dispositions the focus of change. The confessional technologies opened the thoughts and aspirations of the individual to inspection and regulation. Previous church conceptions of revelation were transferred to strategies that produced personal self-reflection and the inner, self-guided moral development of the individual (see, e.g., discussion about religious cosmologies and theories of social change and evaluation in Popkewitz, 1984, 1991). While certain religious notions of change (individual and social) were embodied in social theory, Christian ethics were no longer explicitly promoted but were viewed as embedded in the progress that science brought to social life. The organization of reflection through pastoral techniques did produce moments of doubt and skepticism, but the skepticism, questioning, and problem solving were related to the particular problematic of reason that emerged in relation to the problems of governing.[8]

Reflection replaced revelation in finding human progress. Psychology institutionally replaced moral philosophy to provide a scientific approach to saving the soul (see, e.g., Hunter, 1994; O'Donnell, 1985; Rose, 1989). Discursively, psychology transferred religious confessional practices to the realm of personal self-reflection and self-criticism. Personal salvation and redemption were tied to personal development and "fulfillment," words that signaled religious motifs but placed them in secular discourses of science and rational progress. Psychology makes personal autonomy and individuality "not the antithesis of political power, but key terms in its exercise, the more so because most individuals are not merely the subjects of power but play a part in its operations" (Rose & Miller, 1992, p. 174).

The pastoral power recast the messianic view of progress into a secular culture of redemption. It was believed that personal as well as social development could be purchased. The social administration of the self, as Foucault (1988) and more recently Rose (1989) argue, reenacted early church interests in rescuing the soul through the new social welfare institutions such as were presented in mass schooling.

The modern school was a technology that linked reflection, revelation, and progress to the soul of the individual. The psychologies of pedagogical practice create a therapeutic sense of the individual whose life could be normalized and made constructive and productive. The school brought progress through rescuing the soul using theories and technologies constructed with psychology.

> The school was to act as a moral technology, not merely inculcating obedience, but also seeking to shape personality through the child's emulation of the teacher, through the use of pastoral techniques to encourage self-knowledge and enhance the feeling of sympathetic identification, through establishing the links between virtue, honesty, and self-denial and a purified pleasure. (Rose, 1989, p. 223)

In contemporary reform, the moral domains of the soul are the site of struggle. The pedagogies of learning, problem solving, measurement, and child development regulated not only how information was formed but also the principles by which individuals assessed their personal competence and achievement. The theories and techniques of the pedagogical sciences and teaching bring into scrutiny the innermost thoughts, ideas, attitudes, and feelings of the child. The new culture of redemption ties social policy to the mentality of the teacher, who is to save and rescue the child (Popkewitz, in press).

But the discourses of achievement and redemption in schooling are not what they seem. As we pursue the different discourses of pedagogy in the urban and rural schools of Teach For America, I will argue that the discourses of salvation "make" the child an individual who is not reasonable, capable, and competent but who—with the proper care and nurturing—can be saved.

Populational Reasoning and Social Regulation

A different technology of normalization is the populational reasoning in pedagogical practices. Thinking of people as belonging to a population is so much a part of our "reason" that we are often unaware that our views of people as belonging to a population is a historical invention and the effect of power. Populational reasoning emerged with state reform tactics concerned with administering social welfare (Castel, 1991; Hacking, 1990, 1991).

People came to be defined as populations that could be ordered through the political arithmetic of the state, which the Germans called *statistik*. State administrators spoke of social welfare in terms of biological issues such as reproduction, disease, and education (individual development, growth, and evolution). Human needs were conceptualized in instrumental and empirical terms in relation to the functioning of the state. The notion of population produced a new form of individuality. The individual was thereby normalized in relation to statistical aggregates from which specific characteristics can be ascribed to that person and according to which his or her growth and development can be monitored and supervised.

Populations, once established conceptually, can be measured, organized, divided into categories—using statistical techniques—and dealt within as institutions through techniques of power-knowledge. Applying this calculus of probability, populational reasoning constructs our understanding of the way children learn, of school achievement, and of the social and psychological attributes presumed to cause school failure. Individuals and events are organized and reclassified in a manner that separates the particular event from its immediate historical situation. Populational reasoning normalizes through the construction of averages (and other statistical measurements) and hence the normal/abnormal.

Defining how people "fit into" a group as defined by particular sets of characteristics, then, is more than just a way to classify. It is also a system of reasoning that normalizes, individualizes, and divides. Reasoning about children as populations makes possible a particular type of governance. In the schools where the corps members of Teach For America worked, populational reasoning placed children outside the norms when they were perceived as having "no discipline" in their homes, when parents were defined as not reading to their children, and when students were categorized as behaving in a way that implied that they lacked the norms to learn properly. Each of the statistically organized "problems" located the child who could not succeed in school, and who psychologically lacked the self-esteem for success.

The Alchemy of School Subjects

A different technology of normalization relates to the construction of school subjects. We can think of science, social science, mathematics, and literary studies as systems of knowledge produced within complex sets of relations and networks. The knowledge accepted as sociology or physics, for example, involves particular institutional relations and systems of reasoning about research, teaching, and professional status. Further, what counts as knowledge involves struggles among different groups within a discipline about the norms of participation, truth, and recognition. The norms of "truth," however, are not only influenced by internal dimensions of a discipline. They are produced through alliances with groups external to the discipine, such as with state agencies and businesses interested in, for example, laser technologies or on the social question of poverty. When Thomas Kuhn (1970) spoke about "revolutionary" and "normal" science, in one sense he was speaking of the different stakes that are authorized (and want to be authorized) in a discipline. We can call this set of relations in which the rules and standards of knowledge are produced a discursive community.

The idea that disciplinary knowledge is socially produced is important when we speak about school subjects. The curriculum of schools performs an alchemy on that disciplinary knowledge. The specific relations from which historians or physicists, for example, produce knowledge undergoes a magical change. Whereas disciplines involve competing sets of ideas about research (we can call these as paradigms), school subjects tend to treat knowledge as uncontested and unambiguous content for children to learn or solve problems with. Thus, we can say that there is an alchemy of the "discipline" of physics that breaks it up into, for example, categories of "concept mastery," psychological registers about "cooperative small group learning," and concerns about the "motivation" and the "self-esteem" of children. School "science," "math," "composition," or "art" is pedagogical knowledge that conforms to expectations related to the school timetable, conceptions of childhood, and conventions of teaching that transform knowledge and intellectual inquiry into a strategy for governing the "soul."

Perhaps the alchemy of school subjects is necessary because children are not scientists or artists. But that is not my point. It is to recognize the significance of this alchemy in the governing patterns of schooling in two related ways. First, the complexities and contingencies of daily life are reenvisioned as things of logic. Concepts and generalizations are taken as logical, nontemporal structures that function as foundations from which learning occurs. Even methods of research are assumed as logical entities that follow some rules of scientific method that exist outside of social processes, such as learning "laboratory skills" or interview practices. Thus, it is possible in schooling to talk about children's learning as involving conceptions and misconceptions of concepts, as if concepts were stable and fixed entities of knowledge.

The alchemy that makes the world and events seem to be things of logic removes the social mooring from knowledge. The debate and struggle that produced disciplinary knowledge are glossed over and a stable system of ideas is presented to children.

Yet, when we look at research at the cutting edge of science, we can "see" a knowledge that is quite different from that enshrined in the school curriculum. It involves debates and struggles about what is to be studied and how. Further, the conception of knowledge used by research scientists privileges strategies to make the familiar strange, to think about the mysterious and unfamiliar, and to raise questions precisely about that which is taken for granted. The rules of curriculum are quite different as they privilege the stable, fixed, and categorical properties of knowledge, even in recent "constructivist pedagogies" (see Popkewitz, 1991).

A second function of the alchemy is related to issues of exclusion. This exclusion is different from those associated with the children who succeed or fail in a school subject. The exclusion that I speak about is the construction of a moral order that normalizes the child as different from what is reasonable and capable. The alchemy of school subjects makes possible the alchemy of the child. The treatment of school subjects as fixed and unyielding enables pedagogical discourses to focus on the processes by which children learn or fail in curriculum mastery. It is not the knowledge of the disciplines struggled over. With knowledge fixed, the soul is the site of struggle for norms of achievement, competence, and salvation. A particular child can be placed within a continuum of norms that represents some imaginary line on which the "child" is positioned.

The stability inscribed in the knowledge of school subjects, then, is a technology that normalizes systems that function to include and exclude children, but does not appear as such. Rather, the inclusions and exclusions appear as the "natural" logic of learning or individual motivation. At the same time, the pastoral focus on the psychological qualities of individuals (achievement norms as well as norms about self-esteem) shifts the blame for failure more securely to individuals themselves, as there is little recognition of differential access to the means for "self" expression.

There is another dimension to this production of systems of exclusion. The social distinctions produced in the social disciplines legitimate certain dispositions and sensitivities within an array of possibilities (see, e.g., Bourdieu, 1984). For example, we can think of turn-of-the-century "domestic sciences" as designed to bring particular bourgeois ideas into the working-class household. The scientific theories about the management of household finances, individual health "habits," and ideas about family childrearing linked the social disciplines and political rationalities with the self-governing patterns of urban dwellers. Contemporary ideas about child-centered pedagogies that embody a normalized vision of the "natural" child and of "truth" are created. The emphasis on verbalization and justification in the constructivist classes, Walkerdine (1988) argues, relate to particular gendered bourgeois conceptions.

As the social mooring of knowledge is lost in the alchemy, the economy that enables and disenables subjectivities through the inscription of different rules of participation and action is also lost. It now seems that children do not learn or succeed because of their "being." The urbanness/ruralness of the child disqualifies that child because of the dispositions and recognitions that are outside what is sanctioned as reason and the capabilities of "the reasonable person." The alchemy enables a normalization that no longer works to include/exclude categories of people. Normalizations now work to include/exclude certain ways of being, no matter who you are.

In my efforts to problematize the knowledge of pedagogy, I have discussed different technologies that construct a continuum of values that places children inside or outside the "reason" of schooling. Pedagogy, I argue, functions to govern the soul, with the various technologies of pedagogical practices producing a means to shape and fashion the conduct of individuals. To follow this line of thinking, there are two more concepts that I must explore before moving to the interpretation of the ethnographical data of the construction of the urban and rural teachers. One of these ideas is the spatial politics of knowledge. The second is the scaffolding of ideas.

THE SPATIAL POLITICS OF EDUCATIONAL REFORM

We can think of the "outcome" of normalization processes as producing a space that children inhabit. This inhabited space is not what is conventionally thought as physical, "contextual," or geographical. Rather, the space that I speak about is one constructed through the systems of ideas, distinctions, and divisions. This space, however, is no less "real" than the geographical one. To speak of the child as an adolescent, as "at-risk," or as having "low self-esteem" is to construct a space in which to locate the child. The different ideas provide a way in which to think, speak, see, feel, and act toward the child. The different ideas overlap in a manner that produces boundaries to what is possible in thinking and acting. The discursive spaces function to intern and enclose the child within the normalizations that are applied. Further, as we explore the spaces constructed for the urban and rural teacher and child, there is a spatial politics that functions as a system that qualifies and disqualifies individuals for participation.

A contribution of postmodern social theories is to explore how discursive spaces are constructed and how they operate as systems of internments and enclosures (Popkewitz & Brennan, 1998). Postmodern feminist literature, for example, has explored how the concept of "womanness" has been historically constructed in social spaces and changed over time.

Riley (1988), for example, explores how the concept of "women" has changed over the past few hundred years within European discourses, tying historical texts (discourse) to a particular geographical location (European). Riley traces the changing construction of women over time, ranging from the placement of women in religious spaces as a "soul" dominated by the church, to their insertion into social spaces that visioned/re-visioned women through their bodies and sexuality. Riley argues that the social spaces in which women are located weave through multiple institutions: church, family, welfare systems, schools, health. Riley argues that there is no essential "nature" to the identity of women, but it is an identity that is produced as the effects of power.

In the sense posed within feminist theory, we can think of pedagogical discourses as constructing social spaces for children—theories of childhood, ideas about learning and development, "make" us see the child through particular psychological distinctions and divisions. Our thinking about the child as enclosed in a space of "childhood" is so "natural" that we think that a child has a preadolescence or the "terrible twos" without recognizing that these classifications are socially constructed within a social field of power. We have selectively forgotten that the spaces of childhood are relatively recent social inventions. Even as late as the 19th century, children in schools were placed in a schema that had no representation of childhood. Children were "scholars," not "learners."

The significance of the spatial politics of pedagogy relates to the productive problem of power. Whereas 19th-century social theory and political projects focused on actors who rule or are ruled—what I called the sovereign concept of power—a central problem of power is the spatialization of identities as constitutive of systems of inclusion/exclusion. "Identities" are no longer produced solely through one's geographical location but through a recursive system of recognition and divisions (Wagner, 1994). The urbanness/ruralness of the child and teacher is part of this spatialized politics of governing the soul. Curriculum becomes, from this point of view, part of a discursive space through which the subjects of schooling (the teacher and child) are differentially constructed as individuals to self-regulate, discipline, and reflect on themselves as members of a community/society.

TEACH FOR AMERICA AND THE SCAFFOLDING OF IDEAS

The spatializing practices of pedagogy, however, do not occur from a single set of distinctions but are formed through a grid by which intelligibility is given to actions. I call this grid a scaffolding. The scaffolding focuses on the different trajectories of ideas that come together to construct the "reasoning" and the actions of teaching.[9] By thinking of pedagogy as a scaffolding of discursive practices, this study considers the assemblage of ideas and practices that produces the normalized child. This approach is contrasted with most research, which focuses on a single discourse (the psychology of learning, or management as separate from curriculum ideas). The idea of scaffolding is to recognize that the reason of pedagogical practice is produced through an overlapping of different sets of ideas. The "thinking" and "seeing" are therefore produced through a field of relations in which the ideas are placed. The resultant knowledge of teaching is more than the sum total of the different ideas when viewed separately.

The idea of scaffolding relates to the spatial politics discussed above. The constructions of urbanness and ruralness are produced through different sets of ideas that form a grid from which the teacher and child are "seen" and "see" themselves. Different discourses about "managing," "learning," "caring," and "succeeding" that inhabit the world of schooling come together in the everyday practices as the reason by which the actions of the teacher and children are constructed.

The consequence of the scaffolding is not the sum of the different ideas but the result of the grid deployed in the concrete practices of classroom teaching. Further, the normalization produced includes and excludes— not by the categorical privileging of groups (for example, white versus black or male versus female), but through generating principles by which individuals construct themselves as active, self-motivated persons.

A NOTE ABOUT METHOD

My conceptual focus on the spatialization of the urban and rural teacher has methodological consequences. While it is the speech and actions of various actors in the pedagogical field that provide the "data" analyzed, the interpretation of the data centers on the rules and standards of "reasoning" that organize and position those actors. This focus is sometimes called the "decentering of the subject." The locus is how the actor (the subject and subjectivity) is constructed through particular systems of classifications that organize the objects that a teacher acts on. I, therefore, continually refer to the discourses of pedagogy, and position specific events or people within the subject positions constructed through the scaffolding of ideas.

In one sense, this approach makes problematic what the sovereign notion of power assumes—how reason and rationality socially construct intent and purpose. Intent and purpose are not something applied to social action but are produced through the discourses that "make" possible what is said, "felt," and done. The study, then, reverses the focus on the conventional notions of socialization of teachers by focusing on how the systems of ideas embodied in the organization of teaching construct and normalize the teacher who administers children.

Thus, the following discussion momentarily moves the actors (corps members, teachers, children) "to the side" to consider the rules that construct reason and the "reasonable person." I say "momentarily" because this methodological decentering of the actor is not intended to deny that people act to change the world. In fact, the opposite is true. The consequence of this method is to open the possibility of action through problematizing the system of reasoning that interns and encloses our subjectivities and actions.

This decentering of the subject has another aspect. The research project observed and interviewed approximately 70 corps members, many of whom were of color, and teachers, TFA staff, and school administrators. While there were ideological differences among various groups in the corps, there also was no unity in that ideology within racial and ethnic groups.[10] But ideological statements are not the same as the practical logic of teaching. The logic of practices in the schools had only certain sets of distinctions available about pedagogy, regardless of race, class, or gender. Although clearly there are other distinctions available in academic literatures (see, e.g., Delpit, 1988; Gore, 1992, Ladson-Billings & Tate, 1995; McCarthy & Crichlow, 1993), these alternative discourses did not enter into the everyday discursive practices. Thus, the following chapters focus on the construction of the discursive spaces in which racialized subjects of pedagogy were constructed.

My position may produce a strong reaction as it "hits" an American sensitivity that places a high value on individual initiative and on human purpose in giving direction to social affairs. My concern, however, is not to disregard these Enlightenment sensitivities. My strategy is to recognize that reason is historically constructed and is the effect of power. The doxa, the unquestioned assumptions of existing forms of "reason" are made into the primary problem to be understood. That stance is not to eliminate reason but to explore the particular systems of pedagogical ideas and rules of reasoning as the effects of power in schools.

Thus, this approach challenges the determinism of the world by relativizing and historicizing its ways of "telling the truth" and the "will to know." In questioning the systems governing subjectivities we open the possibility of reinserting the human subject into history by providing potential space for alternative acts and alternative intentions to be articulated.

This methodological approach leaves questions of resistance and contradictions within the discourses of schooling for others in subsequent investigations. My concern is with the system of reasoning through which a space of the urbanness/ruralness is constructed for the child. It is for others, at a later time, to explore the notions of resistance that stand within these power relations. At the same time, interrogating pedagogy as a governing practice is a political intervention and a potential act of resistance.

The organization of the following chapters focuses on the concrete pedagogical discourses by which the urban and rural teacher is constructed. It considers how social discourses are inscribed in pedagogical reasoning; the embodying of pastoral care in the psychology of teaching; the recipe, experiential knowledge of teaching; and the social functions of the alchemy of school subjects. In thinking about these different discourses as a scaffolding, I sometimes return to particular events and interviews to explore the multiple levels of ideas for a grid that normalizes and excludes.

To return to an earlier point: Teach For America provides a point of entrance in which to consider the educational categories and principles that form the *urbanness/ruralness* of U.S. schools. Thus, while Teach For America reform strategies target "inner-city" and "rural" schools to overcome the inadequacies of educational practices, the ideas about inner-city and rural intersect with other ideas about the "troubled" psychological development of childhood, conceptions of school subjects taught, distinctions of intelligence, technologies of classroom management, and views of achievement. The scaffolding of the different ideas assigns values and divisions about the subjective differences of the children. It is the production of this space for children that I explore but that reform discourses leave unproblematic.

Chapter 2

THE SOUL AS THE ACHIEVEMENT
OF TEACHING

THE SOCIAL SPACE OF THE URBAN
AND RURAL CHILD

In Chapter 1, I spoke about governing of the teacher and the child as being not only about the behavioral rules of class conduct but about the principles generated for action and participation. I argued that pedagogy is a normalizing practice in the struggle for the mind and body. The significance of the normalization is that it assumes particular sets of distinctions and classification that "makes" the urban/rural child as different. The function of teaching discourses, I argue, is different from the rhetoric to provide equitable and just schooling. As I discussed earlier, the discourses that make the urbanness/ruralness of the child produce a space that is different from that which is silently present in the classification. Different discourses about instruction, the psychology of the child, the school subjects, and the experiential practices of teaching form a single plane. The resulting scaffolding of ideas produces a reasoning that cannot be reduced to any one of the discourses but constitutes the child in an oppositional space that is different from and outside of what is seen as normal and educable.

This chapter, then, begins the exploration of how different discourses produce the space that is inhabited by the urban and rural teacher and child. I scrutinize how social and political distinctions about the child and community are embodied in pedagogical practices. The inscription of social values is not explicit but is silently embodied in the distinctions and divisions that classify the urban and rural child. One important element in this construction of difference is the doublet. The doublet is a concept that is used to understand how the negative social characteristics assigned to children of color are re-visioned as "positive" characteristics that teachers nurture and develop, thus inscribing the child as someone who is different from what is normal and reasonable. The negative/positive social images do not appear as such but appear as embodied aspects of the child's intelligence and potential.

My interest, then, in Teach For America is to look closely at the discursive practices of the schools in which the corps members were placed. In the following chapters, I examine how the social systems of classification relate with other discourses of pedagogy, such as psychology and pastoral care, the experiential knowledge of teaching, and the curriculum (the alchemies of school subjects). The amalgamation of different discourses is viewed as producing a particular space about the child who is knowledgeable/not-knowledgeable, successful/unsuccessful, and reasonable/unreasonable in schooling. While this discussion focuses on the first year of Teach For America, a program that has since changed, the discourses that populated the schools are not unique to Teach For America. The discourses that construct the teacher and the child as urban and rural are embodied in a scaffolding of ideas that are part of contemporary teaching and teacher education, an issue that I will take up in the final chapter.

CONSTRUCTING THE CHILD: HISTORICAL DISTINCTIONS IN TEACHERS' SPEECH

How are distinctions about "reason" and the "reasonable" constructed by teachers in the schools in which the corps members were placed? I start with an interview with a Teach For America corps member who taught Spanish in a middle school whose students were mostly African-American. The interviewee discussed the complex situations in which teachers and children are placed in schooling.[1] The teacher in question graduated from a private, highly regarded American university and viewed the teaching experience as an opportunity to "give something back" to society for the privileges that she felt she had enjoyed. The corps member works to provide relevant teaching experiences and makes a distinction between the school curriculum designed around textbooks, testing, and school standards and the social background of the children in the school. The teacher argues that the school's educational requirements—such as learning a foreign language like Spanish—do not meet the most pressing needs of the children.

> Students need English. . . . Students . . . need to be able to write simple sentences in English. . . . Students . . . need to be able to carry on a conversation without saying "ain't," or "got none," or any of that. . . . Not every one of my students needs to know Spanish, but every one of my students needs better English skills. Desperately.

The teacher looks for strategies to establish priorities and to make the classroom a more successful learning environment. The corps member adds that the school needs to find ways to redress the cycles of poverty and discrimination through which instruction is organized. There is also a recognition of the institutional dysfunctionality of schooling itself, as the corps member suggests that the best possible scenario is for children "to get through here without being permanently scarred." The questioning about teaching Spanish is tied itself to a feeling that the institution is not working properly through the curriculum currently offered.

We can view this expression of the purpose of teaching in different ways. One is to consider the effort of the corps member to confront the everyday difficulties of teaching and reorder the priorities so as to have a more humane and challenging classroom environment. Seemingly as unquestionably, one can think of rethinking existing priorities about teaching English instead of Spanish as evidence in this interpretation about confronting the difficulties of the classroom.

But we can also consider the distinctions and categories as not necessarily those of the teacher but as historically constructed sets of distinctions that generate principles for the acts of teaching. That is, the priorities inscribed in teaching are not merely personal "beliefs" but historically produced categories and distinctions that order what is scrutinized as the practices of teaching.

Let me explore this historically constructed quality of the teacher's speech through the corps member's statement about "needs." The construction of children as having needs joins a biological metaphor about what is natural to the children with social norms that differentiate children's use of words like "ain't" and "got none." The linguistic differentiation of needs constructs the children of color as non-normal or abnormal in relation to some unspoken norms about the relation of identity to the use of language.

Here, we can begin to understand that the discourse of needs that explains differences is embodied in particular historical discourses. The discourses are mobilized for children who are viewed as outside of normal reason and somehow to be rescued or saved. The "norms" of this reason, if I use the above example, regard certain styles of speech as "natural"; but the "normal" is not examined or scrutinized. The children who possess the urbanness/ruralness come to be regarded as unnatural or not-normal as they lack what is natural. The normalization of children by their use/nonuse of language in the corps member's discussion is not overt but is carried in the linguistic differentiations that divide children.

The description of writing and conversational skills, then, is more than an expression of hope and intent of teaching practices. The statement encompasses a set of norms inscribed in the categories and differentiations that distinguish the children of the class from others who are not present. But the norms appear not as social and political distinctions but as the subjectivities of the children—norms that place the "needs" of children in a continuum of values that establish difference.

The "need" to learn English is enmeshed with other distinctions about achievement, competence, home, and community that construct a social space that locates the child. This grid becomes apparent as the corps member establishes distinctions by which to pursue the problem solving of teaching.

> I didn't realize the background my kids came from. . . . I didn't realize that my background was where I had a safe place where I could go home and study as much as I wanted. Whereas these kids, they're lucky if they can sleep at home, let alone do anything else. Even watch TV. All they do when they're home is have their parents yell at them and have their parents blow smoke in their face from their cigarettes and things like that. They can't study. And the school is just so disruptive. . . . There's so much pressure not to learn; there's so much pressure not to do what's expected of you that the best that most of these kids can hope for is to get through here without being permanently scarred.

While there are contradicting elements in the above statement of the corps member, the pedagogical distinctions construct a continuum of values about what is normal and reasonable. Success is related to the "being" of the child and the home. The successful child is one who can sleep at proper hours, study, and who is allowed to develop self-motivation and responsibility—dispositions and actions that are absent in the children of the class. The lack of English language skills stands within a grid of ideas whose normalization testified to the child's lack of competence and achievement. The students are positioned as anthropological "others" who stand against reason—they "can't study," are "just so disruptive," and are "pressured not to learn."

The children occupy an oppositional space to what is "normal." The nonsuccess of the child is embodied in the normalized capabilities of "being" which the child in the school lacks.

If I move to another corps member discussing the experiences of teaching, certain moral/political distinctions are inscribed in the ordering and dividing practices of pedagogy. A corps member makes a comparison between current experiences and her own growing up. The conversation constructs a hierarchy that links what is good and bad, successful and failing. Referring to the classroom, the corps member says that

It's two totally different worlds. . . . as a military child, we were not
wealthy. We were pretty much middle class, maybe upper middle
class for a while. But my mom's been divorced and so . . . she
doesn't have a whole lot of money, but we were comfortable. We
always had a roof over our heads, we always had a telephone, we
had a TV, we had cable, we had magazines, my parents both went
to college, so a lot of these kids, their parents didn't go to college, a
lot of them didn't graduate from high school. They're very low
income. We're a Chapter I school I think. I'm not sure, maybe
Title I, whatever it is, they're all below the poverty level! Not all of
them, but a large percentage. My homeroom I've got, out of 24
students, I've got 20 of them on free meals, so it's a different world.

In the above statement, success is found in wealth, which makes a
difference in children's learning; but wealth is not alone in constructing
the successful students. Wealth itself is not necessarily important as it is
embodied in a series of "dispositions" that differentiate those who are
educable from those who are not, for this corps member's mother does
not have a lot of money. Being "pretty middle class" does matter, but this
is related to other dispositions that underlie "being" educated, watching
cable TV, having a telephone, reading magazines, and going to college. The
distinction of "divorce/broken homes" functions to normalize the child
further. Divorce is different from the "broken homes"/"single-mother
families" of the children in the school, the latter historically locating the
children's homes (and, therefore, the children) within discourses of social
pathology.

At this point, one might ask: "TFA involves 'the best, brightest, and
most highly educated and privileged among our college graduates.' They
have committed themselves through Teach For America to provide a just
and equitable education. The corps members are put through school experiences that are designed to rescue children, and yet they come out with
these constructions of race and education. Thus, can it be assumed that
schools are hopeless or that teachers are racist?"

My argument here is somewhat different. The very categories "invented" for administrative purposes (race, intelligence, learning, etc.)
merge with psychological categories (personality, dispositions, affect, learning style). In this way, the administrative categories now function at a
subjective and personal level, as evidenced in the merging of social and
administrative categories with those of pedagogy. When corps members
talked about the needs of children, for example, they deployed particular
historical discourses that mobilized to classify and divide those who are
different from the normal. The normal is assumed and made natural as it

relates to what is non-normal and outside of reason. The very discourses of teaching, learning, administration, and teacher education are what populate the schools to make the space of urbanness and ruralness different from what is reasonable and normal.

The distinctions about children's needs are not only "categories" or labels applied to children. The categories are embedded in a range of distinctions and differentiations that form a grid of intelligibility to the world and individualities of schooling. The distinctions stand as an ordered totality by which the shadings of difference are applied to children. The different discourses of pedagogy can be thought of as constructing a field from which teaching is seen, thought about, felt, and acted on. In an important sense, the scaffolding of discourses produces the reason from which purposes of teaching are constituted—what "makes" for a "good" student. Schooling is the production of the rules embodied in action and participation. This opening analyis, then, is to inquire into the scaffolding of ideas whose consequence is to normalize inequality.

CONSTRUCTING DIFFERENCE: DIVERSITY, UNITIES, AND THE CHILD AS THE "OTHER"

The idea of difference and diversity in teaching has gained momentum in recent discussions of how schooling can contribute to social equity and justice. That discussion typically focuses on the groups of people represented in school curriculum and decision making. In this section, I pursue the construction of diversity and difference in a different empirical manner. I examine the social distinctions and differences that are inscribed in the concrete practices of teaching. Specifically, I focus on different binaries produced in the discourses of the teacher. At one end of each of the binaries are the norms of reason and competence. At the other end are the children in the schools where the Teach For America corps members were placed. The children stand in an oppositional space to reason. The two poles divide what is assessed as success or failure in the schools. For example, there are binaries that order the division of children into White/ Black. This division is then discursively overlayed with other distinctions such as smart/dumb, and aspiring/indifferent. The scaffolding of the binaries, however, does not seem as divisions but as a continuum of values in which one side of the distinctions is privileged as the composite "makes" for what is "good" and normal. The construction of the binaries is obscured as universal values are thought to be applied when thinking about all children's achievement and developmental patterns. I will argue here and the following chapters that these universal values presumed to be the same for all children are fictions; the fictions are embedded in pedagogical practices that "make" differences and diversity from the universal norms of sameness.

We can locate the logic of binaries by turning to a corps member's discussion of the problems of integration in the rural southern community where he teaches. The corps member is repulsed by the White flight from public schools as private academies are created. In this discussion, he explains the function of racism by referring to a class analysis of the functioning of schooling. He asserts that

> the whole idea of integration they told me was to raise the quality of Black's education up to that of the White. Now, in fact, what they said was, the Blacks are hauling everyone down. White parents are reacting, pulling their kids out, sending them to private schools. So I think the smart kids in this community are in private schools, not to mention, I also believe anyone in this community with enough money or enough dreams to leave does leave.

The children are divided into two different groups: White and Black. The corps member then reinscribes these distinctions with others to differentiate and explain the actions of teaching: Those who are "smart kids," have "dreams" and "money"—they are educable; those who are Black and have the unspoken but oppositional norms are uneducable. The corps member argues that he had to insert discipline into the class to produce "good practices." These efforts, the corps member stated, had unforeseen consequences as Black students thought that "the teacher must be racist" when a poor grade was given or they got into trouble.

As before, the corps member can be viewed as finding ways to address the social inequities of schooling. In this sense, the statements express a search for solutions to dilemmas that corps members confront in schools. At the same time, there are particular rules of problem solving that make possible the expression of "dilemmas" and the solutions to the situations of schooling. These rules involve casting the pedagogical dilemmas as embodying moral/political distinctions. The social distinctions appear as particular binaries: White/Black, private/public, wealth/poverty, smart/dumb, privileged/deprived, and aspiring (dreaming)/indifferent.

The binaries recast social norms into a continuum of values to classify teaching actions. Differences are produced as universalized norms about what ought to be the same for all children but in which the "urban" and "rural" children differ. When different poles of the binaries are placed, for example, in relation to each other, White/private/wealth/smart/privileged/aspiring have linguistic, normative priority, these poles of binaries standing in opposition to the attributes held by the children of the school: Black, public, poor, dumb, deprived, indifferent, and without dreams. Further, and important to the making of teaching, the oppositional space of the child is administered through certain universal norms of sameness; the universal but unspoken norms of sameness (White, smart, wealthy, privileged) produce value of difference and diversity in the ideas of learning, individuality, and instruction.

But the production of difference involves an asymmetrical relation and a fluidity to the identities established. The normal in the binary is assumed only as a normal constructed to what is non-normal. The discourse privileging the non-normal is something to be characterized, examined, classified, and defined. Thus, it is *normal* to talk about urban and rural schools while having only generalized and undifferentiated categories that stand for schools that are presumed to be opposite and of the norm and average, such as those generalized labels of "suburban," middle class, or White. Further, while it is usual to hear of failure attributed to race when applied to people of color, it is unheard of within education discourses about urban and rural schooling to hear of success attributed to race.

My concern in this book, then, is how the racialization of the child intersects with discourses of class, but also with discourses of intelligence, curriculum, the psychology of the child (one's self-worth), and the practice management of the teacher ("the wisdom of school practices"). The resulting space of urbanness and ruralness is the logical outcome of the historical conjuncture of different discourses in the production of schooling.

DOUBLETS: POTENTIAL AND INTELLIGENCE AS ABSENCES AND PRESENCES

The construction of diversity from norms of sameness is not only about establishing negative spaces from which children of the "urban" and "rural" schools are administered. In the schools of this study, the norms that make differences are also re-visioned as positive attributes of the "nature" of the child who is rescued from the conditions of abnormality. This turning of negatives into positives sounds, at first, counterintuitive. But, as I illustrate below, the negative norms become reversed as the presumed routes of salvation for the child. The very norms that were to enclose the child as being without "reason" function as values to direct successful teaching in the inner-city and rural school. To save children from the conditions of their urban and rural lives, the negative, oppositional poles of "reason" are made into principles of a "relevant" and successful teaching.

This taking of the negative, oppositional pole of what is absent in the child and recasting it as a positive pole to find personal redemption can be viewed as a doublet. The doublet, a double logic that operates simultaneously, is expressed in teaching in the following manner: Norms about the absence of reason in children (the second pole in White/Black, private/public, wealth/poverty, smart/dumb, privileged/deprived, and aspiring [dreaming]/indifferent) are remade as attributes "cultivated" through the teacher's watchful eye.

We can examine the doublet through discourses about children's potential and intelligence. Intelligence is registered as a phenomenon that involves indeterminacies rather than some "innate nature" or universal norm; that is, as recognizing differences in how children express ideas, use language, and learn. As intelligence and potential are talked about, differences in children's achievement and competence appear, rhetorically at least, in instructional programs to maintain a social commitment to equality. The "signs" of children's intelligence and potential attest to the teacher's belief in children and the possibility of their achievement and competence. Children who previously were unsuccessful in school learning can now be placed within a positive, constructive light, thus presuming to counteract the constraining negatives that are seen as defining urban and rural children.

But the defining of intelligence is not an abstract, logical concept but appears within a doublet of absences/presences. If we take the phrase "street-wise intelligence," this doublet is made visible. Introduced by corps members to describe their commitment to "help" students, street-wise intelligence ostensibly differentiates and gives a positive spin to the reasoning of the children. A corps member discussed the children in the class, for example, as having a particular type of "street wisdom" in which intelligence could be identified and learning fostered. The classification of street-wise intelligence was a strategy to support and encourage the children. This corps member argued that the students in his class needed confidence "because these kids are bright, they're so bright and they kind of realize that they're bright."

But the intelligence of street-wise was combined with other distinctions that ordered and divided: The corps member differentiated the children's intelligence as not directed toward academic success but, as he said, "you know. They know they're smart in terms of [being] quick and witty and street-wise and they can always outnumber you in what they say. It's very verbal."

But turning negativities into positivities makes it not possible for the child to ever be normal or average. In the above statement, for example, there is a grid about absences and presences. "Intelligence" and "brightness" are related to other phrases about being "very verbal," "quick and witty." But these divisions are different from "normal" intelligence: The children's intelligence is classified as a wisdom that is different and distinct from that which is normally valued in schools.

Here we can explore a transformation of negativities (street-wise intelligence as distinct from normal intelligence) into principles for positive action. The concept of street-wise intelligence creates normative spaces for action. The teacher is concerned with an unrealized and invisible "intelligence" realized through the teacher's care and attention. At the same time, the street-wise intelligence is different from what is normal and reasonable. The positive space is also the pathological "other," as stigmatized community traits are assumed to be "natural" to the child unless they are stamped out—"[being] quick and witty and street-wise. . . . It's very verbal."

As with street-wise intelligence, the notion of potential counterbalances the negative consequences of schools with an outlook that identifies those aspects of the child's "nature" that can be nurtured and developed. The norms of reason construct the *urban/rural* child as lacking the "natural" attributes of reason and ambition. However, this division creates a dissonance for otherwise there would be no path for redemption. The notion of potential resolves this dilemma. Even if children lack proper intelligence, it is "reasonable" to subject the children to teaching in order to "realize their potential."

But the "nature" in the child's potential is not natural; it is socially constructed within a doublet of pathology and capability. In one school, for example, a corps member reacts to the advice of a fellow teacher who "said to me don't bring yourself down to their level, don't use the lingo, you can't act like them." Reacting to the rejection of the children, the corps member describes the children's "potential." Another corps member referred to a child considered a "discipline problem." He mentioned the potential that this child has, but added that the child "just can't control himself."

The insertion of "potential" is the insertion of a doublet of the reason/nonreason of children. Universal social standards are applied that contain both negativities and positivities by which children are judged and are to judge themselves. The standards are not spoken but are inscribed in the above juxtaposition of "bright" and "discipline problem." The principles of potential intern the child just described as "bright" but having a "natural," inherent quality that, if not remedied, would be "out of control," and create a discipline problem.

In a different situation, a corps member was perplexed by the contradiction between what was perceived as student achievement and vocational goals. Students expressed general goals in life that required doing "well in school . . . they want to [be a] pediatrician, lawyer, you know, all these other types of things." These goals were seen by the corps member as distant and unfulfillable. However, the tensions were partially resolved through the insertion of the idea of "potential." In order for students to be "made" intelligent, potential was linked to norms inscribed in the statement that students must first learn to like school and then acquire the proper attitudes toward academic learning. As a corps member puts it, "And, you know, first, I really, really want them to just like school."

Potential, then, is positioned within a grid of ideas in which the child embodied an aptitude for work, and moral inclinations, as well as the state of the body and of the mind. The struggle for the child is in the subjectivities—to have potential, the children must become self-motivated and self-responsible through "liking" school. It is assumed that with proper remediation, children can exhibit the norms of competence, but these norms of competence are those that shape and fashion the oppositional space of urbanness and ruralness.

Intelligence and potential are doublets of presences/absences. They classify the child as "lacking," but suggest that with the proper "nurturing" and the development of the proper "subjectivities," deficits can be turned into positive qualities. Classrooms are organized to bring forth something unrealized—that is, a capacity or a potential that is presumed to lie within the individual but is not yet visible. Instructional methods are ostensibly intended to help children "develop intelligence." In this way, the child who lacks the "proper" norms to succeed is repositioned on the other side of the doublet—the child who has potential and intelligence exists within the images of the urban and rural space that is classified as different from other spaces.

The doublet normatively transforms the child. The words *intelligence* and *potential* position the child in opposition as the "other" to be worked on and scrutinized as both negatives and positives. The negativity is dissected and reclassified to construct a purpose for teaching. The normal is no longer problematized; it is assumed. Furthermore, that assumed nature constitutes a space that is not attributable to the urban/rural child. The space of "the normal" is socially constructed in a way that makes it impossible for the urban/rural child to be average or normal. That nature is not a neutral biological and deterministic conception of childhood but instead one related to the social situation and indeterminacies of teaching (the potential of the "street-wise" intelligence).

Thus, at one level, the discussion can be read as the inscription of class and race into the distinctions of school success—African-American children are different from what is normalized as "success" in school. But this distinction makes the problem one of the categories of actors rather than how those categories generate principles that order the subjects of action.

The fixing of the categories loses sight of how distinctions and divisions produce and are produced in a field of unequal social relations. If a fixed notion of intelligence were used to describe the actions of the teacher, then it would not be possible to talk about street-wise intelligence or potential. In contrast to a fixed concept of intelligence, the practical reasoning of teaching is contingent and fluid. The "racialized" and "classified" space of the child is produced through the amalgamation of different sets of distinctions that construct "urbanness" and "ruralness."

To summarize to this point, I have been exploring a scaffolding of ideas by which intelligibility is given to the actions of the teacher. I focused on how norms of difference are discursively constructed through norms of sameness. The binaries of smart/dumb, White/Black, aspiring(dreaming)/indifferent, I argued, for example, embody norms of sameness from which the second, oppositional pole of difference was constructed. Further, what seems as a negative element in the subjectivities of the children in the schools is reinscribed as something positive, to be worked on to rescue the child. I called this inscription and reinscription a doublet. The doublet takes the absence of reason in the child and remakes it as a positive presence to attend to through careful and mindful instruction. But the presence of the doublet always makes the space that is inhabited by something that is different from the average, the normal, and reason. Although it seems that this relation of doublets defies our sense of symmetry and logic, the presence of a street-wise intelligence and potential is constructed from what is discursively positioned as absence.

POPULATIONAL REASONING AND THE ORDERING
OF THE OTHER

In this section, I pursue the scaffolding of discourses through the inscription of populational reasoning. In Chapter 1, I argued that populational reasoning produces a particular type of social space in which to understand individuality. It is not uncommon to have children classified as uniform members of populations with particular characteristics, such as children from broken homes, crack babies, children with low self-esteem, and so on. The binaries and distinctions discussed above embody a populational reasoning—notions of children's achievement and capacity are related to distinctions of wealth/poverty, integration/segregation, smart/dumb, Black/White, middle-class/low-income. Populations are what teachers act on! Populational characteristics function as causal associations between a statistical grouping of people and the attributes of particular children, even

though, strictly speaking, statistical predictions have no bearing (no pre-
dictive power) on individuals.

Populational reasoning is part of the commonsense reasoning of teaching. It is no longer deployed solely as state or administrative reasoning but
instead as the teacher's personal reasoning about how to order and identify children. Statistical probabilities appear to be essential individual attributes of a child. At one level, populational reasoning constructed for state
administration of schools is embodied in the reasoning by which teachers
classify and divide children. When asked how many students she had in
her class, a corps member responded:

Corps Member: Well, right now, I have 29. Last week I had 37.
Interviewer: In a kindergarten class?
Corps Member: Uh-huh. So they changed. They moved some over, and
    this, and that—and "that" was just me. . . . I'm half and half. I
    have, out of the 28, I think I have 15 Mexican and 13 African
    American. So it's an even mix. And even though I don't have any
    Spanish background—you know, I cannot speak Spanish other
    than the basics—it's going smoothly.

Populational reasoning is not only about assigning children to groups.
It individualizes the general attributes of populations to particular children
in school through a hierarchy that ascribes a "nature" to students. Children are classified as undifferentiated members of African-American and
Spanish groups that have essential characteristics that ascribe the "causes"
of individual children's actions to the nature of their being. The corps
member who previously rejected the teacher's comment about "bring-
ing yourself down to their level" and inserted the notion of children's
"potential" to direct teaching used categories of populational norms about
the achievement (and nonachievement) of children to define the purpose of teaching.

Populational reasoning inscribes the child into an undifferentiated
unity from which the teacher administers. A corps member who talked
about the difficulties in teaching, for example, asserts that certain basics
are needed prior to being successful in school: "If you don't learn how to
do certain things, you're never going to pick it up." At this point, the corps
member explained the failures of the students by their membership in
particular population groups. "You know, I don't want to say, I don't want
to make it sound like I'm saying Hispanics are lazy."

To make the point, the corps member explores differences by distinguishing between different geographical areas of the city: "You work your
way down to Madison Street, down by 104th and you're talking about apart-

ments and projects, so you've got a much poorer school. So their scores are a lot lower." The concept of "learning to do certain things" is not specified, but is instead used normatively to position Hispanics as "others" who are "lazy." The idea of laziness is part of a trilogy: poor, Hispanic, lazy.

Populational classifications not only establish boundary conditions under which groups are administratively organized, but also provide the classification within which teachers think of themselves and the actions that are open to them. In one high school, a corps member spoke of the school as having "a reputation . . . of being the most intellectually rigorous." The corps member then added that this reputation is "scary" because of the social inequities in which success and failure are distributed in the school.

> I think the relationship is much the same as any in a very mixed area where the school, the Parent/Teacher Association, and all the different organizations that have some effect on how the school runs are dominated by upper-middle-class white parents. The school is most responsive to their demands. I don't think it's because they're rich. I don't think it's because they're White. I think it's because they call and they come in and they give us a hard time if we don't do what they want us to for their kids. [On back to school night, the turnout] was exactly what you'd expect. It was, in the honors class, which is mostly white and upper-middle-class, lots and lots of parents there. In my nonhonors class, [the] very few who came were the parents of the few kids who were doing pretty well.

At one level, we can think of the statement as evident of class and racial distinctions in defining the competence of children. But these social and racial classifications weave together with other sets of distinctions that focus on the dispositions, sensitivities, and capacities of the child. The resulting identities are racialized but in a complex, indeterminate structuring that is fluid and contingent rather than fixed and stable. We can understand this indeterminacy in the discussion about success and failure of children. The inscription of a doublet—the "White, rich parents" versus parents of students in the nonhonors class, most of whom do not participate—involves asymmetrical discourses. The discourse about success of children is related to the individual actions of parents who respond and demand "what they want . . . for their kids." The discourse about failure appears in relation to the foundations of "correct" behaviors built on probabilistic (populational) reasoning that inscribes certain universal moral/social principles about how one should act.

The distinctions and differentiations, however, are not reducible solely to race or class but involve the insertion of multiple norms of the space occupied by the child. The asymmetry of the discourses defines children who succeed in school—those who are generally upper-middle-class and White—as opposed to something that the "other" children are not. But the seeming rejection of the social-class distinctions to organize teaching in fact repositions and links the social distinctions to other unexamined norms for organizing practices—the norms of populational reasoning that define achievement in "honors/nonhonors classes"; the rules of populational reasoning that order parent involvement/noninvolvement provide a greater specificity to the divisions that originally seem undifferentiated, universalized categories of rich and White.

Whereas the normal is embodied in the individual actions of parents who represent "successful" children, historical discourses about the capabilities of children are mobilized, and they function to place the urban/rural child outside reason. The oppositional discourse deploys a populational reasoning that makes the non-normal something to be characterized, examined, classified, and defined through categories of participation and achievement. The normal exists within a complicated web of discourses that are not examined, but are made natural in the ascriptions of what is non-normal.

Probability reasoning in the populational grouping of children occurs not in isolation but within a scaffolding of ideas through which a "nature" is ascribed to the child. This "nature" embodies norms about behavior, linguistic competence, and skills that "make" the educated person (Fendler, 1998). One corps member, for example, described the children in his class as a unified group, and compared them with his own brother who "is as old as these students are and he's like four years ahead of them in his education. Just the way he acts and the way he's been taught and his education—the way he can relate to things."

A series of norms positions the students in a manner that differentiates and divides them from others:

> These students are very backwards and you're trying to teach them out of a book that's geared toward students like my brother, not geared toward students the way they are, with this deficiency and you find that you have to adjust yourself because you lose them they'll become discipline problems in class.

Discursively, the brother is positioned as a normative reference from which to establish rules for understanding competence and achievement in school. But the conception of competence and achievement is in the dispositions and sensitivities needed to be "educated." The children in the school are different from the corps member's brother. The differences, however, are not categorical—e.g., White or Black—but are in the differences of actions, mannerisms, and sense of "being" of the children and the brother. The brother stands as a generalized set of dispositions and capabilities from which to place the opposition of the children of the class.

Populational reasoning is more than an abstraction by which to describe people. While produced as an administrative category to organize social programs, populational reasoning functions as a social practice that historically classifies, differentiates, and divides the urbanness and ruralness of the children from others regardless of their race. As such, I have spoken of populational thought as a system of reason rather than a system of categorizing. It not only provides administrative categories but it relates to other discourses about children's participation, achievement, and salvation. When teachers describe their pupils and classes, they do so, to a large extent, as collections of distinctive aggregates. Populational reasoning regularly provided principles as corps members talked about "the smart kids in the private schools," "the haves or have nots educationally," or the fact that it seemed like the effort to help every student in a large diverse classroom was too great a task, given the "gap in the amount of education that they can absorb." These categories inscribed populational attributes onto individual children as explanations for failure/success. The norms of success and failure are embodied in the subjectivities that enable/disable participation.

THE "SOUL" AS THE ACHIEVEMENT OF TEACHING: CLASSIFYING AND ORDERING THE CHILD

The scaffolding of ideas explored to this point normalizes the child. That normalization is borne through the inscription of a continuum of values that places the "urban" and the "rural" child as standing in a discursive space that is in opposition to what is "reason" and achievement. The binaries, the doublets, and populational reasoning, for example, take the *absences of reason as the presences* that teachers work on and cultivate. But children's intelligence and potential are not of some "natural" ability but are aspects of life that were to be made visible and cultivated to rescue the child in the rural and inner-city schools.

The normativity made the site of battle as the rescue and care of the child. What began as civic responsibility was transformed into a pastoral power to rescue the child. The moral responsibility of schooling is to govern "the soul"—inner beliefs, feelings, and sensitivities that generate actions. One corps member describes the change in relation between teacher and pupil in the following terms.

> [What] has changed is not so [much] the responsibility, just the way I look at the responsibility, since . . . now I'm obligated by law. Before it was this ideological sense in my mind that I wanted to help society. I wanted to hopefully make a change for the future. Now, dealing with that reality, I'm looking at it more as a responsibility—like I have a moral responsibility. Not just a responsibility to myself to teach these 33 kids, but a moral responsibility—like I feel it's all on my hands. I try to be like almost a policeman for the whole school.

The "lack" of capabilities noted as students "not motivated," "not prepared," and "not present in the classroom" is the struggle for the soul. The moral responsibility of the teacher is to re-vision the inner beliefs and feelings of the child.

The achievement of teaching is the moral governance of the identity of the child. When asked about expectations, a different corps member focuses on his shift in expectations from some general sense of knowledge and being knowledgeable to a focus on the "soul":

> Oh, my expectations were that (laughing)—oh, I feel stupid—my expectations were that I would come and just teach; and my students would be so thrilled to have this wonderful, knowledgeable teacher that they would just soak it all up; and I would never have any problems. That they would all respect me, because I was on their side, and because they respected somebody who knew what they were teaching, and all. It changed. My expectations now are that I'll just be able to keep them alive, to keep them from becoming disgusted with education . . . getting to the point where they do feel they can do things.

The discourses of the teacher that I have examined register a certain selectivity and set of distinctions. While Teach For America corps members recognized, to some degree, the social complexities and political contexts of schooling, the discursive practices of the teacher gave focus to teaching as a governing practice that would rescue the child. But that rescue also interned and enclosed the child in a particular social space of *urbanness* and *ruralness*. That space located the child as outside of reason and the normal. The normalization is not stated explicitly or "seen" but is produced through the distinctions and differentiations that order and di-

vide the objects of schooling. While we can think of the subjectivity as inscribing racialized and class concepts, these distinctions relate to other discursive practices through the scaffolding of multiple discourses, and thus
have no single origin.

THE TEACHER AS A ROLE MODEL:
ABSENCES AND PRESENCES

In the above examples, we can identify how populational reasoning shifts
from a category of bureaucratic management to a category of personal
identities. The populational reasoning structures the corps member's descriptions on multiple levels—ordering and dividing what is absent/present
as learning, and school achievement, as well as determining the social/
psychological attributes used to classify success and competence (and failure and incompetence).

The populational reasoning that orders the absence and presence of
reason is embodied in the idea of the teacher as a role model. The teacher
as a role model is part of the common sense of contemporary reform literature, stressing the "need" for children of a role model since their homes
and community are viewed as not providing support for adequate psychological development.

The insertion of the idea of a role model can be seen from a different
point of view—that is, as the effect of power. It imposes a continuum of
values from which the different behaviors and dispositions of children are,
with careful monitoring and moral interrogation, to be brought into consensus with the norms that define the "model." But that consensus can never
be achieved as the scaffolding of discourses produce the doublets and the
populational reasoning which places the child in the urban/rural space.

The notion of role model itself establishes an imaginary "nature" in
which certain norms are inscribed about what children should have but
lack. These norms are to rescue the child so that its "soul" has "morality,"
"fairness," "kindness," and "tolerance." A corps member stated, for example, that "I want to assist them in developing a code of morality for
themselves—of fairness, kindness, tolerance. And I want to serve as a role
model for them." In another situation, a discourse about role models articu-
lates a sense of desire, to bring "hope" to children by becoming a model of
what they needed but lacked. The distinctions inscribed in the idea of role
model appear as general categories but its referent is the countervailing
norms signified by students in the classes.

The idea of role model embodies a moral responsibility to rescue the
child. The teacher as role model assumed a particular outlook about cer-

tain universal values about childhood that would morally uplift students by regulating behavior and manners. By having children model teachers' actions and behaviors, a redemptive quality can be instituted in the child.

Historically, the idea of a role model is a concept of regulation and governing. It is a concept that first emerged in early 20th-century social theory to explain the relations of others as "imitation-suggestion." Imitation-suggestion was "a way of accounting for the influence of a leader or a genius on the public, and the ways in which women and blacks could be marginalized by being deprived of 'copies' of the dominant culture" (Leys, 1994, p. 213). But in contemporary pedagogical practices such as those discussed above, the ideas of "tolerance," "hope," and "role model" were positioned within a scaffolding of ideas that placed the child as an anthropological "other" who was different from what was silently normed. However, the classifications were not only of the children who came to school; the discourse generated the principles through which the corps members acquired the sense of the self-satisfaction and competence of teaching itself.

Again, there are tensions in the "reason" of the corps members that point to multiple interpretations. The idea of role model, like the idea of potential before it, seems reasonable—teachers are to give hope and expression to the redemptive culture of schooling. But as we place the ideas within the particular scaffolding of ideas through which we reason and construct the reasonable urban and rural teacher, certain distinctions and divisions emerge. Here, we must return to a continual theme in this study: The "reason" of teaching, learning, childhood, and achievement is socially constructed on a playing field in which there is an uneven distribution of eligibility for participation and action. This unequal distribution of eligibility functions in pedagogy, I argue, through the assignment of a seeming unity in which differences are constructed. Differences are something that occur through the continuum of values that differentiate, for example, "the brother" from the children of the school, that make "divorce" different from "broken homes," and that take populational thought to individualize norms of success and failure. The imaginary unity from which difference resides "makes" children who do not subscribe to these unspoken norms different and "outside" of the normal.

THE MULTIPLE AND CONTINGENT POSITIONS OF DIFFERENCE AND THE RACIALIZATION OF DIFFERENCE

At this point, the racializing of children did not follow logical lines or consistent norms of differentiation. As I discussed earlier, different ideological sentiments about the purposes of teaching were expressed that did not fall into categories expressed through racial, ethnic, or gendered distinctions. When the discursive practices were examined to understand the constructions of childhood, the logic of practice was more complex than the practice of logic (for discussion of this distinction between logic and practice, see Bourdieu, 1990). Some of the school children, for example, were racialized as they were compared with implicit cultural norms that involved shifting lines delineating the way children were "othered."

The multiple and fluid constructions of the "other" can be explored through a teacher's description of her success in a city school. Gender intersects with a racialized construction of the child and community. In contrast to the corps member who saw Latinos as lazy, this corps member "saw" her teaching as benefiting from the matriarchal system of African-American families. The teacher said that male authority is respected in Latino/a culture, and female in Black culture "because mothers head a lot of the families, so I do feel that is a blessing for me. And they take more kindly to females bossing them around, basically." A different corps member inserts gender into the comparison of African-American and Latino/a children, but with the opposite conclusion. He positioned African-American women as not having "their parenting skills anymore" and inscribed this "lack" to the "kids who are pregnant" and "drop out of school," "making" a particular political discourse about the populational characteristics of inner-city African-American teenage women as essentialized qualities of the family and the child.

In these social discourses about the child is an indeterminacy rather than a fixed, categorical essence to the child. By this I mean that an oppositional space of "urbanness" and "ruralness" is constructed for both Latino/a and African-American children. Both groups of people are discursively positioned through populational categories that focus on unities from which absences and presences are constructed. But the Latino/a and African-American groups are placed within a continuum of values to form the boundaries of the oppositional space. The Latino/a is viewed as educable in one situation and noneducable in another when positioned in relation to African Americans and other groups in the spatialized location of urbanness and ruralness. The boundaries established are not straightforward but are spatizalized differentially through the reason of success/failure in schooling.

The indeterminacy of social norms emerges in a class learning to speak Spanish in a rural high school. The lesson involved using Spanish vocabulary to name the parts of the human body. The 15-year-old students paired off with one another to draw their bodies and label the body parts. One member of each team lay down on a long white sheet of paper placed on the classroom floor. The other student traced an outline of the partner's body. In this exercise the students divided themselves by race but not gender.

The intersection of race and gender was complex, multidimensional, and contingent. A White male student traced his female partner's body by drawing a very general line that showed little shape and very stumpy legs. It was clear that he was disciplining himself in outlining his partner, because of the care he showed not to touch her in any way. His diffidence produced a strong reaction from his partner. On seeing her shape on the paper, she growled and took the pencil to redraw a more flattering body. The four African-American females in the class, in contrast, drew detailed bodies, including details of stylish clothes. This exercise of tracing bodies evoked different styles of expression in which gender and race intersected.

The dividing practices wove race, class, and gender into the production of competence in the classroom. Different groupings of students responded to different types of questions, gave different linguistic emphases, and assigned meanings as they discussed the parts of the body while "learning" Spanish nouns.

The different strategies for drawing and for talking about the body reflected different inscriptions about what was publicly permissible and not permissible—and what was racialized and gendered. The male student drawing the outline of his female partner strongly censored his movements as his hand moved a marker around her body. This censorship embodied gendered, racial, and religious norms in what was possible/not-possible for actions concerned with learning Spanish vocabulary.

Further, the multiple positions and contingencies that defined the groupings were cultural/religious norms. In the above example, religious restrictions were evident in the way students related to their bodies and those of others as well as to the way they thought.

To consider this further, we need to look "outside" body movement and thought to the social context of the school. The school was in a Southern Baptist community where the church prohibited discussions of sex, even though the area had one of the highest rates of syphilis in the country. These religious restrictions were so severe that at a community fund-raising event where three adult White women sang the song "I'm Going to Wash That Man Right Out of My Hair," the women wore shorts and long-sleeved blouses instead of bathing suits. When they were asked about this, the response was that it was not appropriate to show "flesh" on the stage.

The above incidents enable us to understand that the position of the "other" in urban and rural schools entails complex and multiple sets of relations that produce an intersection of race, gender, class, and religion.[2] While my concern in this book is with the political space of urbanness and ruralness, these constructions are multiple, fluid, and contingent—such as the flexibility through which distinctions positioned Latino/a and African-American children in oppositional spaces.

TOWARD THE REASON OF THE TEACHER

This chapter explored a trajectory of the different discourses that produces a way to "tell" what is to be included in and excluded from the thoughts and actions of teaching, what I call a "scaffolding." Not only does the scaffolding of ideas "decree" the limits of "reason," but the scaffolding constructs the urbanness and ruralness of the children. The urban/rural child lies in a space outside the realm of reason and the rational. This chapter began the exploration of the production of the space of urban and rural schooling through examining the inscription of social and political rationalities into the discourse of pedagogy. That inscription interns and encloses the children—binaries of the child, doublets, and populational reasoning "made" what is thinkable and actionable through constructing purpose and direction in schooling. The demarcation of the limits of reason (and unreason), as I argued, is a moral order as norms are inscribed that tie together achievement, competence, and salvation—the norms that govern the soul.

When looked at separately, these ideas might appear innocuous and even neutral as teachers and administrators struggle to help, even rescue, the child. But as I argued in this chapter, when the ideas are viewed as governing principles, an overlay or scaffolding constructs the urbanness/ ruralness of the child. Asymmetrical discourses are inscribed through the rules of differentiation and division. The rules are not fixed but involve a fluidity or continuum when one discusses success/failure and normality/ non-normality in the identities of urban and rural children. Whereas the normal is embodied in the individual, the non-normal is inscribed in populational discourses mobilized to characterize, examine, classify, and define the child who is outside of reason. The normal is not examined, analyzed, or scrutinized, but is made to seem natural only when the non-normal is classified and defined.

In contrast to current literature that talks about teachers' believing in the success of children in order to be successful teachers, this book considers "success" as embedded in sets of distinctions that normalize and differentiate the child through assigning values to the dispositions and sensitivities of the child. Gender, race, and social class are important to this construction of subjectivities, but the social distinctions intersect in a scaffolding of discourses that have multiple boundaries that coexist to normalize and classify.

The spatialized politics of schooling, then, is engendered within the relational ordering and divisions that have flexibility and contingencies that can be schematically expressed at this point as:

1. A space is constructed that positions the "urban" and the "rural" child as different and divided from what is normalized as the "reason" and the "reasonable" students of schools. That is, such children appear by their very natures to be different from, and in opposition to, unarticulated norms that define certain groups of students as lacking the "proper" upbringing to develop "appropriate" cognitive and/or affective qualities.

2. The discourse of schooling also constructs doublets, or double relationships, in which the child's "negative" or "pathological" traits are recast in "positive" terms that guide, rationalize, and racialize how the teacher constructs teaching intended to make the child become "successful" and disciplined. I argued here that teaching practices designed ostensibly to help children develop their "potential" and "intelligence" are discursive doublets that embody the negative norms of the child-as-other while repositioning those norms as positive "traits" from which competence and salvation can be derived. The doublets make it impossible for the child ever to be "normal" or average as the child is interned in an oppositional space.

3. An important element in reasoning of education (and social policy) is populational reasoning. Populational reasoning translates global, probabilistic characteristics of "deviant" populations into personal, subjective traits possessed by individual children. Children are seen as members of statistical groups that possess "pathological" traits that require self-discipline through the intervention of teachers who monitor, supervise, and discipline them "for their own good."

4. The populational attributes of groups are remade into the personal attributes of individual children. Traits such as "poor learning habits" or "lack of discipline" become, through this type of reasoning, psychological dispositions of the subjectivities that must be remedied or "cured" by closely monitoring children's learning. Historically, this discipline of the "soul" was applied from outside through a model of pastoral care, but discipline has been secularized in modern schooling to produce children who can do their own self-monitoring and become "self-regulated" individuals. The psychological individualization of schooling functions as a technology to discipline and supervise the child.

The normalization described here is different from that associated with labeling theories that decry the use of categorical distinctions such as calling a child "at-risk," or the "stereotyping" of groups. The scaffolding embodies rules to organize reason—the distinctions and differentiations through which thought is organized, perception directed, and action constructed. The scaffolding of ideas "makes" intelligible the principles through which the teacher administers the child of the school.

At this point, one might argue that the regulation described here seems too deterministic and, in fact, does not work. It can be argued that all one needs do is go to an urban setting to understand the failure of the regulation of the child. This failure is attested to in the overt attention given to management and student control in American schools, and to the resistance and opposition to schooling seen among many children in urban and rural schools. Further, there are multiple visions/re-visions of teaching, children, and learning that must be considered when thinking about what occurs in schooling. Pointing to what Scott (1990) has called the "hidden transcripts" in social practices, one can always find multiple discourses that operate as alternatives within social spaces but are not authorized to be "heard."

I agree with the above statements, yet argue that what is left unexamined in these arguments about resistance and the "failures" of governing is the scaffolding from which the rules of governing and resistances are produced. The hidden transcripts of children who resist appear within schools rather than standing as alternatives outside of the "othering" spaces of schooling. While I recognize that teachers struggle against and resist the discourses that construct their identities, my strategy is to interrogate the normalizing practices that differentiate and distribute differences; I leave to others the discussion of the mechanisms of "resistance." The rules of reason and intelligibility in school form a stratum of unexamined norms over which other, more consciously accessible debates are layered. It is these rules and standards through which power is deployed and resistance inscribed and that have remained unchanged despite constant efforts at reform that are the focus of this study.

Chapter 3

THE ALCHEMIES OF PEDAGOGY

FROM ETHICAL REGISTERS
TO PSYCHOLOGICAL REGISTERS

The previous chapter began an exploration in the discursive practices through which urbanness and ruralness are constructed. My focus is how differences are produced through an overlay of discursive practices. The differences produced, however, are not what is rhetorically discussed as the problem of inclusion in schools, such as through a multicultural curriculum. Differences are produced through a continuum of values that, at least discursively, establish a particular unity or sameness from which all children are judged. The doublets, for example, reconstitute negative social characteristics assigned to children of color as those of "positive" characteristics that teachers nurture and develop. But the negative/positive social images do not appear as such; rather they appear to be embodied in the child's intelligence and potential. The significance of the doublets, I argued, is that they function to place the child in a space that is to be nurtured and cared for, yet the child is seen as one who could not be of the average. The norms that enclose the child are not named as such but are positioned silently within the discourses of teaching. Further, the differences are of the "soul" of the child—the attitudes, behaviors, and knowledge of the urban/rural child who inhabited that space of the doublet.

This chapter continues examining the scaffolding from which differences are constructed. The discussion of the racialized and class distinctions in Chapter 2 is brought together with other discourses, particularly psychological distinctions that emerged through the interviews and observations in the Summer Institute and schools where Teach For America placed its corps members. First, I focus on a missionary discourse employed about saving and rescuing the urban/rural child. Second, that redemptive discourse is given particular detail through an individualization that relates children's successes and failures to characteristics of personalities, motivation, and self-esteem. Third is an alchemy of school subjects. Teaching curriculum "content" is transposed into technologies for the supervision, observation, and assessment of the normalized child. The scaffolding of the different discourses of mission, psychology, and the alchemy of school subjects involves a movement from ethical discourses about the mission of schooling to a pastoral power concerned with governing the "soul" of the urban/rural child.

MISSIONS, MISSIONARIES, AND THE PROFESSIONAL TEACHER

In Chapter 1, I argued that modern schooling tied religious commitments of saving the soul to the problem of constructing the "New Person." This social administration of individuality, by the end of the 19th century, promoted a schooling that was to "rescue" the child from the moral and economic evils of industrialization and well as to produce the citizen who participated in a liberal democratic society. Schools were to take an untutored, undeveloped intelligence and nurture it. In this process, the child's (and the teacher's) capabilities became the site of pedagogical intervention. The invention of discourses about urban and rural schooling can be thought of as historically capturing that redemptive discourse, but revised and reconstituted through systems of professional classification such as the psychology of the child.

A Redemptive Discourse in Teaching

Historical discourses about the redemptive character of schooling are inscribed in contemporary education as well as in the urban and rural schools of this study. If one reads state policy as exemplified in *A Nation at Risk* (National Commission on Excellence in Education, 1983) or examines teachers' discussions about the purpose of instruction and individual children, there is a continual theme of education saving the nation through the saving of the soul. It is not surprising, then, that the discourses about teaching and school improvement in Teach For America carried a redemptive concern. In the promotional literature of Teach For America during its formative period, a sense of something special was portrayed. That something would enable the participants to go beyond what was seen as normal and everyday about teaching.

The redemptive focus of Teach For America was also to have a social effect on the nation as a whole. Teach For America symbolically articulated a societal "feeling" about the needs and deficiencies of urban and rural schooling. Furthermore, the establishment of a social mission was considered crucial in establishing TFA's organizational integrity, and in establishing its cred-

ibility with the educational community and with the news media and potential corporate funding sources. From the first days of the Summer Institute, for example, Teach For America conveyed a sense of "mission," what
one participant referred to as a kind of "missionary zest." The 8 weeks of the
Summer Institute had a spirit of adventure and excitement underlain by an
implicit hope that the corps members would bring that missionary atmosphere
along with them into their teaching, schools, and classrooms.

At a different level, a sense of mission was incorporated into the discourse of teaching and the teacher. A crops member, for example, talked
about the recruitment of corps members as analogous to induction into a
religious order:

This sense of mission was defined in multiple ways. Some corps members referred explicitly to religious commitment in defining the purpose
of teaching, but structured that commitment through sets of distinctions
that directed attention to the child who was normatively different and in
need of rescue ("My priority is . . . I'm . . . a Christian, I believe strongly,
I have strong faith in God and I believe that he has his kids up there. And
that they need a chance. A lot of chances.")

But more often than not, the sense of mission was that of a secular
concern with social, redemptive change. Corps members felt that their
mission was to correct inequality and to provide paths for social mobility.
Some members "saw" teaching as a type of social activism. Others focused
on the need for schooling to foster individual creativity, imagination, and
motivation. In this way, "learning" would produce greater social access
for individuals and, in the long run, amelioration of the poor conditions
in which the students lived. For others in the program, the commitment
to TFA was a way of giving back to society what they believed were the
privileges they had in growing up.

Again, the multiple senses of mission are not surprising; neither is it
surprising that *mission* was an operative word for the corps members. But
the examination here is to understand how the idea of mission is positioned
within the scaffolding of ideas to give direction and purpose to action. The
sense of mission did not form around abstract principles, but instead coa-
lesced in the pedagogical distinctions and a grid of ideas discussed in this
book to classify the capabilities and achievement of the children.

From Mission to "Professional" Norms of Division

The reconstruction of the teacher's mission occurred, in part, in relation
to discourses of professional commitment. During the Summer Institute,
a discourse about the professional teacher was introduced to link corps
members' personal motivation and perseverance with social ideals and

expectations about equitable schools. The teacher who had professional commitment was viewed as a "force" in developing a workable classroom environment in which children would feel successful and have self-esteem. The successful teacher was viewed as one with "commitment" that expressed both a "passion" for teaching, and the importance of "involvement" in the lives of the children.

As part of the folk wisdom of schooling, such ideas "make" sense. Teachers' sense of mission and commitment go hand-in-hand. They should passionately believe in what they are doing and seek to develop an atmosphere that "engages" children in learning. The folk wisdom also suggests that teachers need to "care for" the children in their classrooms and this caring requires an involvement in all aspects of children's cognitive and affective development. Much educational psychology and teaching theory supports the twin ideas of involvement and passion in the development of successful teaching.

But mission and commitment are not logical or psychological ideas that stand outside of the practices in which they are realized. Mission and commitment embody a particular selectivity of norms, values, and principles that govern action and the participation of the teacher. Some of these were discussed previously, such as the binaries, doublets, and populational reasoning that place children in oppositional spaces. Mission and commitment were also placed within a scaffolding that privileged psychological registers that directed attention to the inner qualities and dispositions of the children.

We can locate the norms that define the mission and the commitment of the teacher through examining the discourses about what is perceived as "real" and practical in teaching. Corps members, for example, spoke about adjusting purpose, rethinking teaching strategies, and readjusting expectations for what could "realistically" be accomplished. The notion of "real," however, is not something "natural" or unmediated; the real was discursively assembled in relation to certain unspoken values about the dispositions and sensitivities of the "normal," educable child to whom the children in the classroom were compared. Thus, one corps member noted that when she started at her school, she had hoped to form "an open, creative classroom, to expose these kids to everything I learned in college . . . to open up their world and eyes. My instinct said, okay, I can do that." However, reflecting on the year in retrospect, she said, "I couldn't."

Expressed hopes and expectations and denied aspirations were recast through a particular individualization of collective norms. The individualization turned the lack of success into the "problem" of the subjectivities of the students who were not motivated and "hard working." Action focused on the inner capabilities that prevented achievement and salvation. The school was to rescue children—to "change kids' lives." The very notion of schoolwork articulated the norms of capabilities and the lack of capabilities. One corps member in a large city directly addressed her feeling of disappointment in the effort she perceived her students were making, saying, "Sometimes I find kids doing nothing—just slipping . . . they're just not doing their work."

The individualization had an ironic quality. The norms of success embodied a sameness from which differences were organized. Thus, when a corps member noted, for example, that he had initially wanted "all to learn," such learning assumed that there was a unified or universal set of attitudes, feelings, and dispositions from which all children engage in school learning. The unspoken continuum of values produced the conclusion that the children of the class occupied some "other" space that was different from that previously viewed as reasonable.

The norms of divisions constructed purpose to action. This is evident in the way a corps member talks about a dilemma concerning her changing commitments to education and teaching. The corps member stated that before she started teaching, she believed that her goals as a teacher should focus on helping students to think critically and analytically. Once she started teaching, she continued, she realized that this focus was inappropriate since, in her words, "I found out how difficult it was to take that sort of approach with students who haven't been there—who aren't used to that."

The norms that defined "critical" and "analytical" became a pole that set aside the capacities of children in her class. In comparison to activities that encouraged critical and analytical thought, the corps member found it "a lot easier to go along with the textbook" than to do other things she had initially found more interesting. The "real" possibility of critical thinking was supplanted by the "reality" of difference.

We can think of this construction/reconstruction of ideals as more than an expression of the individual corps member's thinking. The discursive divisions and distinctions generate enabling and disabling practices. The children in this corps member's class were discursively positioned as having dispositions toward the world that did not allow "critical" and "analytical" thinking. The phrases of critical and analytical functioned as dispositions that positioned the children in this class as "not" having the necessary capabilities. An oppositional space was constructed, inhabited by the "students who haven't been there."

Again, as before, the corps member's construction of her students was not exclusively of her own making, but was inscribed in discursive practices that organized how schools are "seen," talked about, and acted on.

The teacher's shift in "ideals" or "beliefs" did not originate with the teacher but were historically produced as the effects of power. The relevant categories did not originate with individual corps members but instead related to socially constructed ideas about that which is "practical" and "reasonable" and, as we saw in the previous chapter, about "intelligence" and "potential."

The authority given to the normalization produced in the concrete pedagogical practices can be assessed on the basis of discussions about teaching and social inequality. Teachers and corps members spoke about how schooling would correct the injustices of economic and of social practices, but then moved into discourses of pedagogy that separate out the practices of teaching from the social and cultural distinctions that embody social divisions. At no point in the observations and interviews were the very pedagogical discourses of teaching discussed as the effects of power. The normality/abnormality in the reasoning of pedagogical practice went unnoticed except in the broadest rhetorical appeals for a more equitable school and society. Further, while there were exceptions to the above norms of success/failure, a particular specificity was given to the commitment to rescue the child through the scaffolding of ideas spoken about here. To adequately consider the re-ordering and re-visioning of this specificity, the mission of teaching, the discussion turns to the psychological individualization in pedagogical practices.

PASTORAL CARE AND SUBJECTIVITIES AS THE SITE OF STRUGGLE

The construction/reconstruction of ideals involves a double movement. There is the movement of mission and social commitment into "professional" registers about pedagogy—teaching is an analytic task or a task of organizing the classroom around something seen as "real" or "the reality of teaching." The mission/commitment of teaching also entails a movement from an ethical register about the social purposes of teaching to a psychological register about the personal self-realization of childhood. The strategies of self-satisfaction and self-fulfillment in teaching are tied into psychologically derived discourses about the need to maximize human potential, and to produce emotional adjustment and cognitive efficiency. The psychological register also produced rules by which corps members assessed and evaluated their "own" competence and performances.

Child psychology is presented in the schools as theories of child development or learning, but in a form that is overlain with other discourses that form the practical reason of pedagogy. The categories of psychology appear not as formal theories but as distinctions and differentiations that order childhood in the tasks of teaching. The psychology entails an individualization that focuses on particular dispositions and sensitivities of children toward schooling and "self." The psychology focus is one of "pastoral care" where the theological principles of "caring for the soul" are re-visioned as elaborate techniques to enhance subjectivities through self-inspection and self-rectification.

The Self-Discipline of the Child

The struggle for the child's "soul" entails the intersection of different and seemingly contradictory sets of norms. There was the task of "instilling" the correct habits and attitudes. But this instilling also embodied a discourse of rescuing the children from special populations. The latter entailed enhancing the children's subjectivity through making them "self-motivated," "self-disciplined," and possessed of a "positive self-image."

The struggle for the child is illustrated in a lesson on the teaching of history. In this particular lesson, the strategy ostensibly focused on the instrumental goal of children learning "history." The instruction here was about the history of social discrimination, and the representation of people who have traditionally been omitted from the school curriculum. The study was of the Mayan Indians and a story written by a Pueblo Indian. The lesson seemed, at first, to focus on the production of inequities, namely, the destruction of the Mayan civilization and the Pueblo Indian's encounters with discrimination at school.

Within the discussion about the Native Americans' story was a parable about the child who lacks motivation and self-esteem. The terrain for understanding quickly shifted to the way children could and should manage themselves. The corps member's summary of the lesson inverted the focus of the lesson from social studies to that of pastoral care:

> And I hope that they will see that inside of themselves and maybe take it a step further and realize that, it isn't right. People should be treated for who they are inside and their character. I hope that some of them will apply that more broadly.

The history lesson about the Pueblo Indians reformulated social problems into personal issues and personal therapy. The learning of history reconstructed the past into a study of personal attributes and deficiencies. Thus the "history" lesson was a particular history that made social events into moral prescriptions of the "self." The psychology of the child was the subject, an individuality that lacks control, "motivation," and "self-esteem."

In this and multiple other situations, corps members reflected on what children were doing and the difficulties they confronted, but the discursive strategies constrained that reflection which placed the child within psychological registers. A corps member suggested, for example, that even if parents helped, their students would have problems because of their "deficient" personal attributes. "That is, you know, like you can call parents or you can get help but, in the end, you have to get them [children] to do it."

The difficulties of teaching became the lack of student motivation, work habits, and parent involvement. These problems, it was assumed, could be solved by working with students so that they could become "more enthusiastic" and feel more secure in the school setting.

The categories of "motivation" and "self-esteem" transfer the problem of pedagogy to personal, inner-resolve, personality, and seemingly natural—even biological—characteristics. "Children's problems" are no longer social, institutional, or epistemological. Instead, children have "problems" because they are personally lacking in some way. They lack motivation, self-esteem, self-discipline, and so forth. The teacher patrolled the governing of the inner, psychological dispositions of the child that merged the mind and nature: A corps member said that he needs to learn more about "why kids are the way they are. Especially middle school kids because they're so hormonal. You know, they're up and down and up and down."

The mixture of biological and psychological discourses produces an asymmetrical fluidity to the constitution of the child. Normality and abnormality are both natural and indeterminant. The "hormonal" nature of the child's problems makes the abnormality determinate in the *urban/rural* space that the child inhabits and, at best, a teacher can tame and enclose the abnormality. The psychological categories of motivation and self-esteem provide an indeterminacy to that "nature" that can be cared for, nurtured, and made self-governing and responsible, but never outside of the normalities/abnormalities of the urban and rural space that encloses the child.

In a different school, a corps member talked about the problem of instruction as the inner subjectivities of the children that embody dispositions in opposition to what enables success. Such difficulties were confronted in a classroom in which most of the children "could not" do what was expected of them. "50% . . . don't do what I ask them to do. And I do not know how to make a kid do something." The corps member continued that he kept "trying to figure out why they are that way." At one point in the interview, a discourse about school achievement was introduced to locate the "problem" as students' "lack of motivation and stuff."

The psychological register was not only of cognitive limitations but tied to the discipline of pleasure. Different types of "motivations" were tried: Teachers wrote the names of students who finished assignments on the board, and gave them "rewards."

> I'm very big into rewards. I brought them candy, I bring them chocolate, I let them go out the last period. I'll let them do art or anything they like doing, I let them do it. Or I let them see a movie, something like that. Because I can't force them to do it, but I can reward the ones who do it and even the ones who say they don't care, after some time, they start caring.

In the above examples, a particular psychological discourse is mobilized to explain success and failure. Motivation and self-esteem are linked to the body and the pleasure of the "self." The site of battle is the inscription of dispositions, sensitivities, feeling, and caring as the child acts.

Psychological Management: Disciplining the Classroom/Disciplining the Child

Much pedagogical literature views classroom discipline and classroom management as a procedural concern that functions to provide a "good" classroom climate and as an enabling practice of the teacher's administration of instruction (such as sending a child to the back of the room, or removing a privilege like going to the playground). Even certain critical pedagogical literatures accept the distinction of good classroom management as a central category for defining good teaching. But as with the other discourses of the teacher discussed here, discipline and the management of behavior are embodied in a grid of practices from which the urban/rural child and teacher are constructed. The two senses of management, which are otherwise treated as analytically different, converge in the concrete discursive practices—teaching-as-management, which focuses on the organization of lessons and classroom behavior, and teaching as managing the personality, attitudes, and beliefs of individuals, which forms part of the grid of "reason" of the teacher.

The "commitment," the "passion" of teaching, the importance of "involvement," and the normalized child were woven into descriptions about managing classrooms. A corps member noted, for example, that her commitment had to be supplemented by classroom management techniques if she was to overcome the skepticism of her students toward school.

> [If] you're not committed, [and] you don't have that passion, then you're going to have classroom management problems. . . . If you're committed to really teaching and you have that passion, the

kids will sense that. And that makes a big difference. Because they can tell when somebody's in the classroom and doesn't really care about being in the classroom.

Teaching was to help students overcome psychological difficulties. In an in-service program offered for teachers, one of the program's leaders interpreted the difficulties of the classroom as the lack of development of children's inner characteristics: "Sometimes [a child's problem] it's just personality. Get them involved with the special guidance counselor."

Teaching as psychological management was sanctioned in a number of ways that interrelate with previous themes. For example, a psychiatrist lectured to corps members about combating racism through introspection, thereby posing the political issue of teaching in terms of individual reconstruction. In other situations, discourses of teaching focused on the classroom as a place where the weaknesses/deficiencies of children's upbringing could be overcome. The classroom was a place to transmit "wholesome, caring values and traditional ethics." One faculty member at the Summer Institute, reflecting on the possible contribution of the corps members to teaching, focused on their role as being models of caring:

People here are going to be wonderful teachers because they care about the kids. And they are going to stand up in the classroom, and for the first time these kids are going to see somebody that actually does care about them. Because these people do. I've heard enough people talk passionately.

The register of psychology produces norms of redemption by focusing on "the soul" of the child. The goal of teaching was to give the students "a lot of positive reinforcement." The reinforcement embodied a particular view that connected the reasoning about the personal self-management of the child who is self-disciplined.

The most helpful approach for me is a behavioral approach. I mean you just tell them exactly what they need to do in the simplest way and because my kids, they don't get into the long explanations of how or why. It just doesn't work for them. They just need to know exactly what they need to do and what they are doing wrong. It's like your hands are up there, your hands should be down.

Even a discussion of multiculturalism, brought into Teach For America as a way to address the social responsibility of teaching, is practically reformulated into a psychological register. Multiculturalism was understood as a means to produce self-motivation and self-esteem. Thus, one faculty member during the Summer Institute addressed the relationship between a background in psychology and the ability of faculty to help the corps members to deal with teaching.

> I think they need more people among the faculty with a psychology background. Much of what was said in the context of multicultural-ism has psychological implications, and a lot of times matters were absolved simply due to a lack of expertise in the room.

The object of this reflection and questioning thus turned toward the psychological "well-being" and management of the child rather than to-ward the social systems in which these principles of childhood were being constructed. The issues of racism, sexism, and multiculturalism seemed to turn to issues of self-awareness and attitudes. They were not social, politi-cal, and historical problems; they were psychological problems.

One might respond that psychological, pastoral care is a necessary part of schooling. It is important that positive conceptions of self-image and self-esteem be sought where conditions of poverty and racism have pre-vailed. Pastoral care, it would be argued, is necessary to counteract the negative experiences that have confronted children. Much educational literature does in fact suggest that the probability of success for children in urban and rural schools is minimal and that practices should "help" children believe in themselves and in their self-worth. Furthermore, the complexities of modern life have made psychology important in reducing alienation and producing affiliation. We live in a culture of psychology in which it is not unusual for reforms of teaching and teacher education to privilege the personal in order to deal with social issues.

While I recognize the continual tensions of psychology within the "helping" professions, the pastoral caring is produced in relation to other discourses as the urbanness/ruralness of the child is constructed. The ideas of self-esteem and classroom management are embedded within a scaf-folding that divides, distinguishes, and produces a child who is interned as acting outside of the normal and reasonable. The child is made into an object of the teacher's practices as well as a subject who is expected to "patrol" his or her own boundaries by learning and imposing self-discipline. Issues of power are turned toward a self-inspection and self-rectification that affect the teacher as well as the child. The psychology of the child, then, is not a singular, particular discourse about self-esteem, but is em-bodied in a scaffolding.

Within this space the best these children can hope for is to become like the *normal* person. Thus teachers discipline children's attitudes and emotions so that they learn to renounce a set of populational characteris-tics ascribed to them as personal psychological characteristics.

The Pedagogical Reform of the Child Through Pastoral Care

Historically, the technologies of "knowing oneself," acts of "self-fulfill-ment," the "maximization of human potential," emotional adjustment, and cognitive efficiency have been aligned with social objectives and state plan-ning in the 20th century. This is what Foucault called "governmentality." The routes of modern salvation in the modern school are overcoming "backwardness," realizing "potential," replacing what is "lacking" in the child, and building "self-esteem"—technologies of pastoral care to moni-tor and self-monitor. This relation of state planning to the pastoral care of the child is now part of the doxa of schooling itself; that is, the unques-tioned assumptions through which practice is organized.

Schoolwide programs existed that aligned social objectives with the soul of the child. These programs are discussed as providing remediation prac-tices to erase the "cognitive" limitations of the child through erasing the psychological deficits that prevent the child from succeeding. These pro-grams, two of which are discussed below, assumed state rationalities to order the problem solving approaches to classroom teaching and remediate the difficulties that children face in schools. These special programs functioned as "pull-out" classes where children in a school were identified as in need of remediation. The remediation sometimes had a "content" focus, such as learning to read. But that overt focus on a school subject was coupled with and usually subsumed within discourses of remediation that embodied a re-visioning of the subjectivities of the child. The goal of special programs is the psychological rescue of the child through the reconstruction of his or her inner capabilities and dispositions.

Project Attainment and Crusade are exemplars by which to explore the combining of state planning, the problem-solving discourses of teach-ing, and the inscription of pastoral care.[1] These programs were installed in the school to help children develop self-esteem and to find relevant learning experiences in order to provide the children with success. But the concrete pedagogical discourses normalize the child in a space that is dif-ferent from that of the "reasonable" person. The programs are technolo-gies that normalize the "othering" of the child while producing a self-monitoring inner "self."

On the surface, Project Attainment seems to be a natural way to pro-ceed because its purpose was to help children "see" themselves as "suc-cesses" rather than as "failures."

> My first priority within the first two or three months was first of all
> get these students to have a positive self-image. They are not
> dumb. "You are not dumb" I tell them. "You are not stupid. All you
> have to do is work a little harder." I work on that constantly

because I could see tremendous improvement in my students just because of the fact some of them belonged to the project.

When we inquire further into the categories of understanding created by Project Attainment, the notions of self-image and self-esteem is tied to norms about a child's potential/lack of potential and psychological worth. The distinction that the child is "not dumb" or "stupid" stands within the grid of norms about "street-wise intelligence" and "potential," and that children fail because they need to "work a little harder." It is the inner qualities of the child that are the object of scrutiny and supervision.

In a different city, the civilizing discourse of the child expressed a religious focus. A corps member understood teaching as reversing children's dysfunctional behavior. This teacher made reference to a school program called Crusade. The title of the program tied teaching to the idea of schooling as a missionary process. The program was intended to help the child develop a knowledge of the "self." That knowledge inscribed global behavioral characteristics in the children's homes and communities as dysfunctional. The distinctions played a normalizing role, as the descriptions of students' homes as places where "everybody screams; everybody's yelling" provided norms counter to what is achieved in school.

The "missionary" qualities inscribed in teaching need to be seen in a historical context. Before the early 19th century, children professed their faith in religious contexts. Since the 19th century, when mass schooling became common, children have been urged to "profess faith" in a new, secular context. However, one can still see religious traces in the discourse of schooling. The call for teachers to "help" and to "care for" children, so that they can develop a proper "self-image" and "self-esteem," brings pastoral imagery into the schools. The teachers' need to help and to care for students is also discursively related to a particular scaffolding of ideas associated with pupils' self-management.

Instruction as the Inscription of Systems of Trust

The psychological discourses of teaching are employed to develop trust systems. The management of children entails disciplinary techniques that call for teachers to develop systems of trust and security.

Teachers are the "nurturers," "guides," "friends," and "role models" spoken about in the Summer Institute and in the school placements. This positioning of the teacher can be viewed as part of the development of systems of trust through which pastoral care is inscribed. A corps member, for example, discussed the need to be positive rather than negative when seeking to develop classroom discipline. "And what I decided to do then," the corps member said, "was to, instead of always looking and telling them what they're doing wrong, reflecting on the positive and those who are doing [the right things]. . . . But once they started getting more positive reinforcement and they thought they were being rewarded, then it wasn't as hard."

The school itself was normalized as being different from its outer environment. It was seen as a safe, secure, and psychologically supportive environment for children who live in a harsh environment outside of the school. "I want [the classroom] to be a nonstressful, friendly, encouraging community."

RECONSTITUTING SCHOOL SUBJECTS INTO PASTORAL CARE

Pastoral care also provides a way to understand school subjects. What seems on the surface to be a classroom organized to teach curriculum content, is actually a workplace for technologies for the supervision, observation, and assessment of the child who is normalized as deprived of such learning. School subjects are re-visioned as subservient to rescuing the child. It is not physics, grammar, or history that is taught. Subject content is re-visioned in the spaces designated as places to work on the *urbanness/ ruralness* of the child. That re-visioning is one of pastoral care that links discourses about competence and achievement to discourses about personal salvation—what produces personal satisfaction, inner success, and personal reward. Pedagogy transfers curriculum into psychological registers that make the subjectivity of the child available to surveillance, and administration.

A physics lesson can enable us to explore the alchemy of curriculum into pastoral care. The discourse moves quickly from the teaching of physics to the subjectivities of the children. Foregrounded is the "background" of the child as what makes or unmakes learning. The curriculum is the background to the moral order that defines students. The discourse is about how students from "neglected, deprived, and sometimes depraved" circumstances are to discipline the self. The construction of the problem of teaching, for the corps member, is to help children develop their personalities through a step-by-step psychological process of reforming the child's identity. Instruction entails questions of children's dispositions, attitudes, and feelings. Classroom conversations, the corps member stated, are important because "we are just sharing that we're in this together. If we're ever going to turn any of it around, we need to do it on some minute basis." Emphasis is placed on developing social behaviors and psychological atti-

tudes that are "not found" in the students' environment outside of school
life. The discursive practices established normative links between the home,
a universalized "community," and the child who was "rescued." The norms
placed the children and their community within a system of oppositions
that respectively produced or prevented school competence.

The reflective techniques of teaching relate norms of the capabilities
of the children to divisions in school curriculum. A corps member, for
example, assumes the children "tell you the right answers and will not do
the wrong thing, but in their daily lives, you know, the example is different." Reading, studying, and learning physics have little to do with learning that school subject, but are recast into psychological problems of teaching proper social behaviors.

> Ultimately, the most important thing is to learn how to get along
> with other people, I think. I mean, I think that that's what education
> can teach you, that's what literature, especially literature, social
> sciences, all those things in the end, hopefully, you know, learning
> can lead to understanding and if you're understanding someone, you
> know, I don't think you're going to be antagonistic or hateful.

This discourse positioned the children as objects to be acted on concerning norms defining average, optimum, and normal. The teacher "corrected" the deficient traits in students' personalities. Experience with students, the corps member said, is one of talking with the students who are
"from neglected, deprived, sometimes depraved backgrounds and what
leads to that kind of trouble." The rescuing of the children may come late
in their lives as the "elements of an evangelist and an emotional appeal"
are likened to a "coach's pep talk at half time," but that appeal is one more
accurately defined as "late in the fourth quarter."

It is in saving the child "late in the fourth quarter" that satisfaction
and purpose are given to teaching. For the corps member, the saving of
the child "is the most difficult and the most draining and also the most
rewarding experience that I have."

The reflective techniques make the habits, attitudes, and dispositions
of the child the school subject. Affective/moral dimensions join with the
cognitive. This "task" was succinctly summed up by a corps member who
said that "these kids" need "appropriate habits and attitudes and practical
knowledge and skills, I mean I think appropriate habits and attitudes are
so important."

This re-visioning of school subjects as pastoral care is expressed in the
answers to a question asked about corps members' best lessons. Responses
were not reflective of the intellectual content of what was taught. The

reasoning about successful lessons wove together ideas of what it meant to teach school subjects, social reasoning concerning community pathologies, and child psychology. A science lesson, for example, was to induce children to express their inner thoughts and emotions.

> Well, I think [the best lesson] would have little to do with physical science. It's the lesson [in which] I use my genuine caring for the students that I've come to love and as we share and talk about emotional issues and social issues. . . .

Teaching was a strategy to gain the "correct" norms for attaining school learning and achievement. Teaching was to contain or reverse the norms that are classified as operating in the child's home and community.

The discourses inscribe certain global populational attributes of the family and community as personal attributes of the child. The idea that a given child's home and community were or were not deviant becomes the norm to classify school performance. A corps member considered the difficulty of teaching, for example, as caused by the dispositions that children acquired in their homes. Children do not have the correct training because "you know, they go home and everybody is screaming at home, you know. Everybody's yelling. They're just not taught that's the way you act, you know. And if they don't get it at home, and it's a shame that they don't, you know, but they need to." The social images that divided the children stood as "truthful" statements that functioned to interpret children's actions.

Psychological observation and supervision are the disciplinary technologies of pastoral care. Certain socially constructed differentiations and oppositions were re-visioned as psychological categories possessed by the child.

The ordering principles that objectified the child also objectified teachers who reflected on their actions. The racialized and psychological logic that constructed the child was translated into principles that classified teaching. The particular context of the "family" was defined in terms of universal populational characteristics linked to the psychological makeup that produced students' "troubles." Psychological discourses constructed distinctions between the community children lived in and the school "community" that generated the principles by which the teacher acted.

LEARNING NOTE TAKING AND THE INSCRIPTION OF REASON

In Chapter 1, I spoke about curriculum as an alchemy. A particular, formal logic is given to how children are expected to order and solve academic problems. Here I want to interrogate empirically how that alchemy functions. In particular, I consider how curriculum moves from learning school subjects to pastoral discipline through the inscription of the rules for mastery of school subjects.

Embedded in the way that children are to "problem solve," and to find the answers to the problems of the curriculum, are principles to order that knowledge and its understanding. These principles are labeled learning of social studies, mathematics, or sciences, but are principles of the alchemy. As with the medieval grammar learned as part of the trivium to learn the rules of God, the strategies to learn history, science, and grammar are similar to learning the rational order of things. Ambiguity and uncertainty were denied or replaced with a world that was ordered and unyielding. The rules that order knowledge are also those that order the children's understanding of self and the world in which that self is realized.

School subjects are viewed as embodying a particular sequence and order in problem solving. The sequence and order provide entrance to the wisdom contained in the curriculum content. In one sense, the curriculum procedures of problem solving are the elixir of learning. Learning school subjects involves internalizing the procedures that order knowledge. Further, the rules of problem solving classify the world into the rational and the nonrational.

The rules of problem solving and rationality in school subjects are elucidated in a high school lesson on note taking. This lesson was based on an assumption that the ordering and categorizing of words provided rules for knowledge and understanding. Learning note taking is learning the rational ordering of things. The corps member said that when "I'm teaching them to take notes, I'm teaching them to try and think a little more on their own." Students took notes about atoms "so we held up our models and we went through how many electrons and protons and neutrons each atom had and why that made a different element and things like that." The notes that described the subcategories of atoms were placed into a hierarchical ordering of the different categories. The relations among the categories was seen as encompassing the knowledge of science, and the ordering principles of note taking were the practice of scientific methods that ultimately led to understanding.

The process of taking "correct" notes was viewed as embodying the rules of logic that underlay the problem solving that produced all knowledge and truth. The students were expected to take notes in a way that organized different elements and subcategories of information into a hierarchical order. This view of note taking became a "natural" process of solving problems. The nature of "reason" was functionally defined as a taxonomical thinking that administratively classified and "rationally" ordered things. The discursive practices of lessons make it look as if the discovery of "truth" consisted mainly of learning a "pure logic" with which to understand and classify the world.

The rules that organize and regulate school subjects become a self-knowledge that signifies children's competence and subjectivity. This subjectivity is expressed as students' needing explicit directions.

> The students want explicit directions—the page number, the paragraph to read so they can know exactly where they can find it. If it's not in boldface, forget it. They don't read their textbooks when I ask them to.

But the rational ordering of curriculum knowledge is not only of the child's construction of the world. It also invades the teacher's rules of interpretation and justification of action. There is perceived to be a universal standard of knowledge that can be assessed in determining achievement and success—but an indeterminacy in the subjectivities of children who are to achieve the standardized knowledge. A corps member, for example, applied a notion of universality when differences were produced in the classroom. The corps member was accused of racism by some students because, as she saw it, she sought to apply universal standards to each student. The rules of teaching were to help children debate differences through applying the rules of debate and argument. The social and political issues, while real and pervasive at one level, were discussed in class as resolved through the rules of debate and rational "convincing" of the merits of solutions.

> I bring up the subjects and I'm trying to turn the class around where I have a debate where I'm not saying things, but they're saying things. During the whole racism thing, I never lectured. All I ever said [was] is this a valid argument? How I started it was I had people go up to the board and then I said you two are White supremacists, you two are Blacks or Latinos or Asians. Now, tell me, try to convince me [of] your side. And that's how I started it. And they've always asked me how do I feel and I've tried to avoid that.

The corps member continued that she was annoyed when the students in the class called each other "nigger" but believed that the resolution of racism was through dialogue in which rational arguments prevail over those of value or ideology.

M[y students] have made several racist comments. [But] I don't let
my kids say nigger in the class. They constantly refer to each other
as nigger, but I won't [allow] things like that. I've never even
heard [racist comments] in a class. Like we were talking about
Chinese people today. . . . They were talking about how all Chinese
people look alike and they all cook really well. We were just
discussing it.

While the "dialogue" was rhetorically defined as promoting an analytical, value-neutral process, it had multiple functions of normalization.
There are rules of displacement involving what constitutes an argument
and, therefore, what is disqualified because it is not rational or logical.
According to this set of culturally specific rules, rational argument is expected to displace conflict through focus on the rules of logic. It is assumed,
in this model, that instances of failure and social antagonism can be worked
out discursively through dialogue. In moderating this dialogue, the teacher
is assumed to be able to occupy a "neutral" role. The corps member involved in this incident acted as a neutral teacher or moderator while students talked about differences between blacks and whites.

The way of understanding the rules of dialogue and argumentation
made it possible for the corps member to see herself as maintaining an
effective and neutral role in an indeterminant situation, even when students saw the interchanges taking place as being racist. In this way she
was able to say, "[I] think I'm pretty neutral. I think that I'm effectively
neutral. . . . They think I'm racist. But just to see a little discussion, I believe, helps."

The rationality inscribed to order reason, however, is a double inscription that deploys divisions and power. The discourse divided the world into
the rational and the nonrational; these rules are not only external to the
dialogue but embodied in the children. Those who did not follow the rational ordering were outside of reason itself. The principles of classification in the discourse position the African-American students in opposition to certain unspoken norms. Similarly, the descriptions of the Chinese
who "look alike," are inserted into the "discussion" in which differences
are constructed from some norms of unity and sameness (the Chinese "all
look alike," and their essential capabilities are embodied in their cooking).
What seemed to be rules of logical persuasion in arguments also positioned
some outside of reason and some as souls to be saved.

The idea that reason is rational, hierarchical, and taxonomic inscribes
a specific type of normalization in the tasks of the teacher. The view that
reasoning is based only on "pure logic," as Walkerdine (1990), for example,
has argued, historically bestows gender, class, and, in this case, racial iden-

tities. The different practices of logic that we have seen are not merely "flaws" of reasoning among the corps members but are, instead, constructed within a scaffolding of ideas through which the teacher "sees," feels, talks, and acts on the objects of schooling.

GOVERNMENTALITY, PASTORAL CARE, AND THE SOCIAL SPACES OF URBAN AND RURAL EDUCATION

At this point, it is useful to look at the principles of pastoral care in the context of Foucault's (1979) discussion of governmentality. In Chapter 1, I spoke about governmentality as a link between the governing of the modern state and the self-governing of the individual. In the 19th century, the tactics of the state were brought into everyday life through the art of governing. State tactics of reform entailed not only rational institutional change, but also an individualization and psychologization of social problems through a range of strategies, including the development of pastoral care. One part of the construction of governmentality, Foucault argues, was a re-visioning of the notion of family and power. In the 17th century, the sovereign saw power as a downward movement. The prince's relationship with his territory was likened to the father's position as head of a family.[2] By the 19th century, sovereignty referred to a double movement. The family became a subset of populations that could both be managed and urged to self-manage in relation to state tactics of reform. The invention of the modern citizen who embodies particular sets of obligations was a dimension of this shift.

I refer to this genealogy to recognize that modern schooling inscribes the power relations in governmentality. The governing of the child is also the governing of the teacher. Pedagogy is the promotion of subjectivities through "the construction of pleasures and ambitions, and the activation of guilt, anxiety, envy, and disappointment" (Rose, 1989, p. 208).

Pastoral care makes personal thought available to supervision, observation, and administration. Discourses about competence and achievement are linked to ideas about personal salvation—what produces personal satisfaction, inner success, and personal reward. The struggle for the soul is inscribed in the school programs that "care for" the inner subjectivities of the child, the teaching of note taking, and the alchemy of physics. The soul "cared for" is the child divided from what is normal and reasonable. Technologies of schooling produce the deliverance of the child's soul by remaking the subjectivity.

But this consideration of the effects of psychology in governing the teacher must be placed within an overlapping or scaffolding of ideas that give intelligibility to the practices of teaching. The scaffolding of discourses produces a moral order that is both prior to and a condition for the transmission of competence in the practices of teaching. The teaching of note taking objectified the child or the teaching of physics entailed rules of social interactions, classification, and personal identity.

Again, we can "read" the various expressions of corps members in this chapter in alternative ways. We can consider the corps members' reasoning as a series of pragmatic responses to schools mired in social inequities. We can also recognize the virtue of making the classroom a "model" community. Other interpretations can focus on corps members as miseducated, and engaging in stereotyping behavior and/or bad judgment.

While I recognize all of these possibilities, my analysis has continually sought to place the discursive practices within TFA in the context of an amalgamation of practices through which reason and "reasonable people" were constructed. The idea of school as a model community and efforts to remove the stress from teaching and learning, as examples, occur within the particular selectivity and divisions that inscribe a moral order. That order is not external to the teacher or the child but is, instead, inscribed in the patterns of self-reflection and self-consciousness through which the teacher acts. Furthermore, the systems of ideas in which the child becomes someone "who has to get along with others" is not just a statement about the social interaction of children. This phrase inhabits a world of dualisms, normalizations, and hierarchies that embody oppositions between the home-as-community and the school-as-community. The principles for ordering teaching reinscribe social and economic categories as belonging to individuals' identities.

Chapter 4

THE WISDOM OF
TEACHER PRACTICE AS
A NORMALIZING TECHNOLOGY

Previous chapters have examined overlapping discourses through which the urban and rural teacher and child are constituted. These discursive practices, I have argued, are the effects of power through the construction of diversity. This diversity, however, is not what is considered in current reforms but is embedded in the inscription of social and political distinctions in the pedagogical principles of classification. The space in which the child resides is not publicly defined but is performed as the social principles in pedagogy relate to other discourses such as those of psychology and pastoral care. The teaching of physics and "note taking" discussed in Chapter 3, for example, enable us to consider the focus of pedagogy as the soul of the child and not the content to be learned. The construction of the urban and rural space produces a racialized child through the distinctions, differences, and divisions applied.

In this chapter, the discussion moves to the teaching methods and technologies that organize classroom practices. Learning how to plan a lesson and the conceptual distinctions that guide instruction are such technologies. They combine methods and ideas to fashion how a teacher implements the tasks of teaching. Thus, in this chapter I explore how the previous discourses of the teacher come into contact with the technologies that a teacher applies as the practical, experiential knowledge of "good teaching." In the schools studied, for example, pedagogical methods were thought about and acted upon through distinctions about "hands-on" teaching, different "learning styles," the "wisdom of teacher's experiential (recipe) knowledge," and "lesson planning." I explore these distinctions through continually returning to previous examples in order to consider how different discourses weave together into a single stratum of unexamined norms.

I consider the distinction of "practice" and "theory" in the teaching and teacher education of the program as part of the scaffolding that constructs the teacher. The practice of teaching is privileged in the interviews and observations, but this privileging of experience and practice is not about something that is purely practice but is action embodied by conceptual distinctions that order, normalize, and divide action in the construction of the urban and rural space. Practice does not stand outside of theory but is itself a theoretical concept that "tells" one how the world is to be held together and reflected upon.

The technologies discussed are important as they are also very much a part of current reform practices that identify the expert knowledge of the teacher to identify successful instruction. The categories and distinctions of teaching constructs the space of the urban and rural child and over which other, more consciously accessible debates about school reform are layered.

RECIPE KNOWLEDGE AND THE WISDOM OF PRACTICE: ENCLOSING THE SPACE OF THE TEACHER

There is a long history in schooling and teacher education of a particular kind of recipe knowledge that values "doing" over something defined as "theory" or abstract thought (Mattingly, 1975). Such practical knowledge can be viewed as "recipe knowledge" as it seems to define what is "necessary" for present and future pragmatic purposes in schools through making a separation between theory and practice (for a discussion of this type of knowledge, see Berger & Luckmann, 1967). The recipe knowledge of teaching continually gives reference to the technologies of managing the classroom and to the everyday experiential knowledge by which the teacher orders and controls instruction. The value given to the recipe knowledge of schooling is continually reiterated in the distinctions between "theory" and "practice" as well as in the ideas of "relevancy" and "role models" discussed in earlier chapters.

The technologies ascribed to teaching are not just procedures to guide action. The conceptual apparatus that organizes the technologies of teaching is, in one sense, an instrumental, procedural knowledge about how teachers organize the classroom. The hidden curriculum literature of the past decades, drawing on the work of the German Frankfurt School, has given much attention to this instrumental reasoning (see, e.g., Carr & Kemmis, 1986). It has considered how moral and ethical concerns are separated from the organizational concerns of implementing goals, thus repressing more creative thought and goals of social change. This chapter, in contrast, considers the recipe practical knowledge producing action through providing principles for participation rather than repressing action and thought.

The normalizing effects of the technologies of the practical wisdom of teaching can be explored in two examples from the Summer Institute. One is an in-service program for Los Angeles teachers to which corps members were invited. The second is a Summer Institute lesson on the technologies of teaching geared to the corps members.

Corps members were invited to attend an in-service day program on the University of Southern California campus. One of the sessions was led by two teachers from a district high school who had received a lot of publicity about that school's innovative program. Approximately 200 people, many from the school district, attended. The focus of the session was "successful management." On the chalkboard was written: "Who's to be a boss?" and "Establish a stimulating learning environment." The discussion began with specific teaching techniques: "You should be positive. On the first day, for example, you might say, 'I am glad that you brought a pen,' and then explain to them their homework."

The teachers then discussed other techniques that they thought would "empower" students. One teacher volunteered:

> I have the Jeopardy game that kids play. It contains trivial questions about common knowledge. I have them try to tune into their reading and the newspapers. They can get 25 points. They have one minute to answer all of the questions. They love the quick quiz. We have to make the assignments clear and precise. For example, we have homework rules written all over the classroom.

In the above example, there is an overlap of discourses between the technologies of teaching and psychological management. The storytelling about the technologies of teaching is linked to rules about the norms of competence and appropriate principles of reasoning for children. The linkage is embodied in norms of the in-service program, which predicate the problem of classroom management on some conception of how children learn and how intelligence is practiced. The references to "clear and precise assignments," "homework rules," and "quick quiz" are not only organizational practices to order classrooms. They also embody particular sets of assumptions about the nature of intelligence of the children that seemingly does not allow for ambiguity, uncertainty, and unpredictability. In its place are clarity, the definite, and the predictable. Children's "thinking" required that teachers learn the "tricks of the trade" to give order and stability to the classroom.

But the problem of discipline is no longer solely that of the child but also of the teacher who administered the practices of the classroom. The teacher said, "I'm neat. I'm organized, I must be in control. I have at least three bold print signs around. No Walkman; no gum chewing; three times you get a U." The second instructor/teacher interrupted at this point and said, "You need to deal with the consequences. Tell parents and guardians the consequences if they don't do their homework."

The discursive strategies that sanctioned the psychological management of the child also sanction the technologies that manage the teacher. Discussion about motivating students quickly turned to specific strategies that provide classroom control. One of the in-service teachers commented: "There are some students who don't care about schools. If you give them a U, so what?" Another teacher answered: "I put them in the corner like a child. That takes care of them." The first teacher then said: "Sometimes I use scare tactics. I set a tone. I tell them they are the prisoner, I'm the judge, prosecutor. And also the prison guard. I also like to spread a lot of humor around."

At one level, the in-service program seemed to impart practical information about "what works," and was based on the assumption that future teachers can best learn their craft through the telling of experience. The construction of teaching is an instrumental, neutral procedure of classroom management and producing order. It is that and more.

The telling of the "practical reasoning" is a storytelling about teaching. The tasks of teacher training give priority to how the teacher manages the child and "childhood" in order to teach academic content. The storytelling abandons any possibility of intellectual work unless that work can be defined instrumentally. But the emphasis on "what works" establishes a particular way of reasoning about action, "childhood," and children. At the same time, instrumental procedures construct the "mental" capabilities of children by abandoning any possibility that children might want to learn in any but the most limited manner. The child is normalized as having an intelligence that needs "clear and precise" information, fusing mental abilities with those of the body ("No gum chewing") and the disciplining of the "self" (the analogy to the discipline of a "prison" and the use of "humor").

The value of the "wisdom of practice" was not an aberration of the in-service program but was embodied in the discourses of teaching. It was captured in multiple sites of schooling and in the training of teachers that occurred during the year. A corps member, for example, rated the faculty in the summer program by emphasizing the importance of their experience, since they "help us to see where we want to go, and clear the way for us." Another corps member expressed the belief that the institute's faculty should have included more teachers: "Because those who were here who are teachers . . . come with a wealth of information and knowledge and understanding about what really works."

The recipes and practices of teaching, then, place certain boundaries on what is acceptable, "normal," and reasonable in the classroom, and also what is unacceptable, abnormal, and unreasonable in schooling. Particular sets of norms are privileged through the "wisdom of practice" and concerns about the psychological management of children. It is here that we can consider how "purposes" are socially constructed through principles generated to enable teachers and students to participate and act in school. In this sense, practice is not something organic to teachers' activities. But in a more important sense, the experiential reasoning of the teacher is an effect of power. The divisions of reason and the acceptable embody the normalized, spatial boundaries of the child classified as "urban" and "rural."

TECHNOLOGIES OF PEDAGOGY AND NORMALIZATION: THE LESSON PLAN

One of the premier technologies in the administration of teaching is the seemingly mundane task of "learning" to organize lesson plans. The lesson plan is part of the folk wisdom of teaching. It is typically a way to order what the teacher wants, does, and achieves. The teacher states the objectives of a lesson, provides a sequence of instruction that leads to fulfilling the objectives, and then adds some evaluative scheme to assess the degree of success in the teaching exercise. But as with other practices, the technologies of the lesson plan "make" sense because of the grid around which the "reason" of the teaching practices is normalized. In the schools of this study (and important to the construction of the urban and rural teacher), the technologies reformulated social issues into universal procedures through which the apprentice teachers learned "to be" accomplished professionals. The lesson plan ordered and divided the capabilities of the teacher who (was) administered.

We can trace the construction of the teacher through teaching technologies emphasized within the Summer Institute "learning community." This group of about eight corps members and a faculty member (a university teacher of teachers) met on a grassy spot outside one of the buildings on the USC campus. The faculty member, a teacher educator, wanted to teach the corps members the skills for organizing and implementing elementary school lessons. The faculty member asked if each of the corps members had prepared a 5-minute lesson and, on getting nods of agreement, asked each corps member to "give" the lesson to the other members of the group.

The overt emphasis in the lesson planning was on the sequence, timing, and organization of instructional practices. One corps member began the discussion by saying that she wanted to do something useful that would teach about the environment: "Let's pretend we're 5- or 6-year-olds. Everyone be obnoxious. What did you find in the environment?" At this moment, the corps member revealed pieces of paper and other litter remnants she found around the campus. The group talked about the production of garbage and pollution in a modern society. The corps member concluded that it is everyone's obligation to clean up the papers and litter found on the ground. She said, "Let's everyone clean up, then we can improve the environment." The group rose from the grass and policed the immediate area and then came back to the spot on the greenery.

After a nod from the faculty member, a second corps member introduced her art lesson: "We'll draw a well-proportioned face." The student teacher said that she had actually taught this to third and sixth graders. "I have a mathematical formula and diagrams to show how you should proceed. It can guide you so you can be exact and successful in making a face. For example, put the eyes in the middle of the head, not toward the top." The group continued with the directions until each had drawn a face. The corps member concluded by saying, "I got that from a book that had 100 ideas about how to teach."

The third lesson was about juggling. It was rewarded by a broad smile on the face of the faculty member at its end.

The fourth lesson concerned the Alaska oil spill produced by the running aground of the *Exxon Valdez* tanker. The corps member talked about the background to the spill, focusing on the relaxation of tanker safety rules by the U.S. Coast Guard, pressures from oil companies to reduce costs, and the human drama of the *Valdez* captain, who was viewed as caught in the entanglements of others. The lesson was a lecture, but at the same time it was an interpretation of current events and conveyed a strong feeling about injustice and immorality in public policy.

At the end of the presentation, the faculty member ignored the content of the lesson to focus on process and the organization of time. She said to the corps member, "You are real passionate about this, aren't you?" Then, without any interruption, she said, "We need to keep on time, or not everyone will present their lesson."

The problem of the teaching, she continued, was the technologies through which teachers use "visual" aids. Referring to previous lessons, she said, "I'm happy to see the number of presentations that we have. It's nice to see how many visual aids we have and we can think about what it really means."

This was followed by an appeal: "Let's be critical. What does it mean to be visual, anyway? Visual is like entertaining. You promote interaction. You articulate how to use visual style. It's a process that's vocal and visual which, if used correctly, makes learning quicker."

The faculty member then summarized the various lessons. "Let's see what I wrote down about these lessons, it's important that we take notes so we don't reinvent the wheel every time we want to do something. Here are good things that I saw." She began to go through her notes:

> You explained things. You spoke clearly. You chose your vocabulary well. You worked through it in a logical fashion. You were imaginative. You maintained eye contact. You demonstrated good models of what you were going to do. You gave a rationale. You had ongoing learning in some of the practices. You responded well when things occurred that were unanticipated. You were showing something about yourself. You were a good model.

The lesson about lessons provides a point of entry into the particular selectivity of the teaching technologies. There is no discussion, for example, of the use of formulas to teach art. Nor is there any discussion about the individualistic assumptions that underlie the "environmental clean-up" lesson. The pedagogical issue in the *Exxon Valdez* lesson is, if anything, the need to keep to the time sequence of the class or to have a proper organization and performance that, quite simply, uses "visual aids."

We can see that the lesson did not only teach technique or technologies of teaching. The teacher educator's focus rendered the intellectual content (substance) of the lessons inconsequential. Substance was subordinated to pedagogic form and style. "Teaching" is then construed more as managing time than engaging in knowledge production. The "lesson plan" is assumed to have a natural sequence and procedure in its organization of thought and practice; yet the ordering of lessons is neither natural nor merely procedural. It is part of a historically derived logic and "reason" of schooling that emerged in the first years of this century to administer and supervise teachers by rationally organizing their work.

Ironically, the lesson on lessons had no visible child or childhood, as the child was present only as an undifferentiated object. Recipe-based knowledge and "practical" discourses make the norms of the child less relevant than the norms of procedures that were universally applied in good teaching. But this nonpresence of the child in the discourse of pedagogy was a chimera. The techniques of lesson planning inhabit a space with other systems of ideas about the inner capabilities of children—the rules of lesson planning and visual aids inhabit the space where other systems of ideas exist and rub against other ideas about the kind of child who could achieve/not achieve in school, and who could therefore be "saved."

TRANSFERRING SOCIAL ISSUES INTO PEDAGOGICAL THEORIES OF EXPERIENCE

If I ask at this point how it is possible for the teacher to inhabit and to administer the space normalized for the "urban" and "rural" child, one part of the answer is this: through the theorizing that values the experiential knowledge of the teacher without recognizing that this theorizing is a normalizing effect of power.

The technologies of managing classrooms are functionally separated form the public social commitments about teaching. This does not mean that there was no talk of making schools equitable places; neither does it mean that there were no values in pedagogical practices. At one level, one can think of the terms *urban* and *rural* in the discussions of school reforms as expressing concerns about social and economic inequities, and the racism that exists within schools.

But a strange thing happens with the inscription of the urban and rural child in pedagogy. Two distinct types of statements emerge. One type of statement is about the social issues that are to be addressed in teaching. These statements focus on the public commitments that should be given attention in teaching, such as making classrooms relevant, respectful of diversity, and corrective of social inequities. At the same time, there is a practical discourse that provides the technologies for making these general purposes an actuality. The general reform literature in education assumes that this practical discourse is consistent with the general goals of education and mostly focuses on how to make pedagogy more efficient and successful. To put it differently, the reform discourses focus on what is represented but not on the rules of representation.

Yet, what I have argued throughout this book is that purpose and intent are invested through the practical reasoning of pedagogy that produces distinctions and divisions. The discourses of pedagogy produce divisions that set the urban and rural child and teacher in a space that is different from others not specified. This spatialization generates an unequal playing field in the sense of qualifying and disqualifying children for participation. The focus of this research, then, involves the specific discourses and technologies addressed in the tasks of teaching, rather than the formal declaration of principles and commitment. In effect, I argue that the scaffolding inscribes "purpose" as the oppositional spaces of urbanness and ruralness are constructed, with the consequence that a practical reason is produced that runs counter to the public expressions of purpose.

The reversal of public intent is evident in the Summer Institute and subsequent school placements. Issues of poverty, urban realities, and race are discursively shifted through the rules of reasoning about the personal, psychological "care" of the individual, the technologies of ordering classrooms, and the recipe knowledge to teach school subjects and to manage children.

One place where this inversion occurs is in multicultural discussions. Ideas about inclusion were reformulated through practice into seemingly neutral concerns with psychological categories of "learning styles" and ways of organizing an "effective" and "proper" lesson.

Even when the rhetoric of pedagogies within the Teach For America schools gave reference to empowerment and the need for an antiracist curriculum, pedagogies were constructed in a manner that positioned children of color as a unified and undifferentiated population whose "differences" were in opposition to particular norms to which they could seemingly never ascribe. The intersection of race, class, and gender was questioned by corps members, such as differentiating between African-American women and men, and working-class women and professional women. A staff member, for example, wondered whether people of color who had come from wealthy backgrounds could "understand the situation in the urban centers in the United States better than Whites." For her, "the critical divide in the United States is around class not race." A corps member related the problem of racism to class. She said: "Education for multiculturalism was like counseling—[to tell] how [this] racist society really dealt with minorities. Kids with wealth don't deal with class."

The statements of social commitment and mission are reinscribed and revisioned through the discursive systems discussed that classify and order the teacher's teaching. There was no sustained set of distinctions by which to relate questions of race and class, for example, to the principles of representation and division that organized pedagogy. Teaching entailed an alchemy of social issues into issues of the technologies of pedagogy. The discourse about organizing the lesson plan was not an anomaly of the reason of teaching. The lesson plan about the use of "visual aids" discussed previously embodied the reflective principles for the construction of the reason of the teacher.

Thus, while there was a continual recognition that teaching involves social values and issues, these concerns were discursively separated from the practical procedures to organize and normalize the actions of the teacher and children. Where pedagogical discourses were viewed as problematic, that view focused on the "beliefs" about children that teachers held, but not on the discursive rules that normatively compared and divided children. The practical rules that classified and made "known" the child and teacher were rarely if ever questioned.

THE "HANDS-ON" TEACHER/CHILD: THE CONSTRUCTION OF DIDACTICS

In Chapter 2, I focused on the inscription of social categories in the practices of pedagogy. One of the discursive practices discussed was doublets. The doublets were not part of the official discourses of teaching but were embodied in the ways in which the teacher ordered and divided children, such as assigning categories of intelligence and potential. The doublet produced principles of reason that operate both as a negativity and a positivity in constructing the child whom the teacher administers. Here, I return to the idea of doublet but through the more formal, official concepts that guide and interpret teaching. My use of "official" is to direct attention to an explicit conceptual apparatus that circulates within teaching.

Two conceptual distinctions are discussed in this section—the concepts of "hands-on" teaching and "learning styles." These conceptual distinctions about children and teaching seem, at first glance, reasonable ideas about responding to differences among children. When the concepts of hands-on teaching and learning styles are placed within an overlay of other discourses that constitute the urban and rural child and teacher, the concepts embody a particular selectivity and normalization. The concepts function as doublets similar to those described in Chapter 2. But this doublet functions to enclose the teacher who is in the urban or rural school. The "negativities" of home, of childhood, and of community become a space that organizes the principles of success for the teacher who works with the child who is "the other." Thus, what is offered as salvation to the child and the teacher in urban and rural schools is the reinscription of negativity that interns and encloses. The doublet that constitutes the child also constitutes the teacher.

The phrases about teaching through hands-on activities, and phrases about children (and also teachers) with different learning styles, appear as a universal logic that is applicable to all in the school. The phrase "hands-on teaching" is rhetorically related to a maxim of Dewey's pragmatism and progressive teaching. Hands-on teaching implies that one learns by doing. Over the years, curricula in science and social studies, for example, have been organized through activities that focus on inductive and discovery approaches.

My concern here, as previously, is more limited and is focused on how such phrases as hands-on teaching inhabit the places that are spatially organized as "urban" and "rural" schools. In these contexts, the hands-on child described in much pedagogical discourse is one who cannot deal with abstract relations and who learns best by doing specific and taxonomic tasks. In relation to the hands-on child we can also understand the hands-on teacher. The idea of teachers' learning by doing is one that historically reaches back to the turn of the century as a valuing of the "craft" traditions in teaching. When this idea is brought into the contemporary school sites of this study, the "phrase" is part of an amalgamation of normalizing practices that are different from those of the turn of the century. The hands-on teacher learns through practice rather than through the mind. The hands-on teachers and children are concerned with the immediate, and reflection is tied to knowledge that is technical and specific. Thus, the hands-on teacher is discursively enclosed and interned in a space that also is normatively inhabited by the child.

Hands-on teaching is part of a folklore brought into the education of the teacher in the schools of Teach For America. It is captured in the idea of teaching as "being practical" and the continual discursive constructions of "useful," process-type knowledge.

The discourses of the hands-on teacher are also privileged in teacher education. To learn by doing would eliminate theory and provide a more successful strategy for instilling classroom discipline. A regional coordinator of Teach For America, for example, expressed the goals of the corps as follows:

> I want them [corps members] to concentrate more on [a] hands-on approach. It was too theoretical last summer. Like more what's a lesson plan, more how do we handle discipline, more what's a cum file, more what actually is the first day of school. Let's simulate the first day of school. No, we do not do any class work. Maybe you do class work, depending on your students. How do you juggle handling, like 30 children in your classroom and they're all different reading levels? How do you handle that? How do you handle a classroom with 80% LEP, limited English proficiency students and you have no aide? What do you do? It's got to be more practical.

The focus on practicality brings us back to a desire to teach less theory and have more hands-on training. Yet we can immediately locate the desire to "be practical" not as some notion of the natural experiences of the teacher, but as a particular normalization of the capabilities of teachers as well as children. The notions of "reading levels," "limited English proficiency," "lesson plans," and "discipline" in the above statements are socially constructed systems of ideas that construct differences from which teachers work. But these distinctions which function as norms that divide go unexplored.

We can think of the governing of the teacher as we did earlier with the governing of the child—the promotion of subjectivities through the "construction of pleasures and ambitions, and the activitation of guilt, anxiety, envy, and disappointment" (Rose, 1989, p. 208). The discourses about hands-on teaching and management join with discourses about classroom participation and children's "enjoyment" in the educational undertaking—how the mind, body, and desire are connected in pedagogical acts. When enjoyment became one of the primary objects of instruction, for example, success was indicated by the degree to which students "felt good" about the lesson, and whether they "participated" actively in the lesson and its attendant discussion. Instead of asking about the substance of the participation, hands-on teaching emphasized that concrete activities would increase pupil involvement.

One corps member observed, for example, that her best lesson was a half-hour treatment of what she called "affixes." She had wanted her pupils to understand how a word could be changed by having something added to the beginning or the end, so that they could use prefixes and suffixes. In elaborating on the reasons why she considered this lesson a success, the corps member referred to her "worst lessons [which] are when it's a teacher-guided question and answer lesson—a nonparticipatory lesson." The criteria of evaluation were procedural and instrumental, not substantive.

The technologies of hands-on teaching are part of the scaffolding that constructs the image of a child who needs to be patrolled by the teacher. The discourse of the hands-on teacher and child is not only about learning "content," but also the "self"—how and what to enjoy and how to follow the rules for participation and action. Merged are achievement, competence, and salvation for the teacher and the child, tied through the joining of "enjoyment" and participation with the rules of "doing" to learn.

But the enjoyment and participation are inscribed in the spatial politics through which the normalizations and oppositions of the urban and rural child are constructed. The "nature" of the teacher's reason about classroom organization is tied to the discourses about the "nature" of the child's "being."

The reasoning about classroom practice and management is also to reason about the child who is taught to learn specific, sequential, and taxonomic information—through hands-on instruction.

But I mean for example, I know my students don't know how to study. They don't know how to study when you say go home and

study this. . . . And they don't know how to take specific information and process it in their minds. If they've learned something, it's
from having done it many times. They're very hands on about
learning. But, you know, there's a certain type of learning that has
to be mental. Something that they just have to know. Like the
multiplication tables. You've got to know what six times five is and
a lot of them just don't know it. And that's really one of my goals,
just teach them the discipline of studying.

While there were moments in which recipe knowledge was challenged, the discourse of practice and recipe knowledge defined the boundaries of what was acceptable in learning to be a teacher and being successful as a teacher. The technologies that made the hands-on teacher were
inscribed in the space by which success, competence, and salvation were
secured. The construction of the reason of the teacher invokes a discipline
of the classroom that will break yet normalize the disjuncture between
home and school discipline. That space interned and enclosed the possibilities of schooling.

SCALING DOWN: THE CONSTRUCTION OF DIDACTICS

The hands-on teacher is linked to "scaling down" the curriculum. Scaling
down, a term that a corps member used, refers to the expectations, goals,
and purposes that "map" the possibilities and achievements of the child.
    During the school year, there were continual statements about the
reorganization of curriculum in relation to unspoken norms about what
the child possesses (or fails to possess) in terms of the proper "reasoning"
to learn. A corps member characterized the curriculum of the classroom,
for example, in the following terms:

> I've kind of adopted sort of a very bare-bones curriculum. Like,
> there are a few essential things I want to get through—get them to
> know well—and the rest of the stuff some of it I'm not even doing
> because they won't use it immediately, and if they're not, they'll
> forget it. So I'm trying not to do—not to teach—for exposure, you
> know. I'm trying to get the very essentials in.

The discourse about a "down-scaled" curriculum is more than an ar-
ticulation of standards about learning. What is selected as curriculum is
related to the subjective, personal success and competence of the children.
The "bare-bones," down-scaled curriculum brings with it an assumption

that there is some unspoken "base" of information and formal, analytical ability in intelligence that must be taught, and that the curriculum embodies at its minimum. The scaling-down positions the child, once again, as being "rescued." The child to be rescued is, in some way different from, even oppositional to, something that is "standard" and "essential" to another set of "normal" children. To speak about the "few essential things I want to get through" relates school curriculum knowledge to norms about the child who thinks, acts, and feels as a competent "being."

The scaling down produces a spatial reason to the urban and rural school, child, and teacher through connecting the curriculum with the appropriate teaching. The curriculum separated the school knowledge from the child. The children are characterized as "lacking" or as having a "limited fund of knowledge" on which to base learning.

The discourse assumes knowledge as stable and unified, involved with universal systems of information that children have or do not have, and are ready or not ready to learn. For example, a corps member working in New York attempted to adjust the curriculum to the "level" of pupils by incorporating an explicit model of bits instruction into his teaching. As he talked about teaching science and mathematics, the corps member said:

> What you have to do for them [in] everything you teach them is break it up into very small bits. Like if you're going to do prime numbers, you have to break it into these numbers and these numbers. . . . Everything these kids do needs to be broken down so simple . . . [and] they need to emphasize those simple terms before they know what they are doing.

Here are moral as well as cognitive "structures" to organize actions. Since the problem affecting the children is envisioned along a continuum of academic preparation/nonpreparation, working with those who had "poor academic preparation" demanded that extra preparation time would "solve" the problem of school nonachievement. Thus, corps members believed that they should work harder to make "themselves" more effective and to correct the "unpreparedness" of students. Corps members gained reputations among other teachers and administrators for putting in long hours at both ends of the school day.

A certain problematic about teaching is thus inscribed. The corps members worried about working hard enough, and about their personal adequacy for the task at hand; however, they were also concerned about the amount of time that their teaching took from the rest of their lives, and about the exhausting nature of their work. A corps member addressed each of these issues, saying:

If you work hard at something, you should be able to do well in it; and I can't. I'm just worried that I'm screwing up the kids. . . . That, maybe, they would have learned with a different teacher, and they're not going to learn with me. It's kind of like there's not enough time, and there's some kids I know if I could work with them real intensively I could get them [to do] so much better. And then I'm not trying hard enough, you know. I just get so exhausted; and then I don't try.

It is significant that the notion of academic unpreparedness, which seems on the surface descriptive or a "merely" cognitive standard of achievement, is also normative. The notion of "academic unpreparedness" embodies norms that order and classify children's inner capabilities. The above discussion of learning, ability, feelings of disappointment, and "slipping" embodies unspoken norms about the successful/unsuccessful child. The distinctions remained unspoken, but served to define and divide the teacher's sense of personal competence and achievement.

The reconfiguring of expectations and the standards to "rescue" might be understood as a response to the anxieties corps members felt about their ability to teach effectively, and the instability that is a hallmark of urban schools (Bruckerhoff, 1991). But the notion of academic unpreparedness, for example, was recursively brought back as a norm to classify competence, as well as principles by which corps members could assess their success as teachers.

But the norms of achievement, competence, and salvation of the child embody norms of the teacher as well. In the fall of their first semester teaching, a corps member—who could have been speaking for many of them—said:

I think in one way it might have hurt at the beginning because I was so danged set that I was going to cover a certain amount of material—because I thought I could do it. And I thought, well, I know the subject well enough; I should be able to do it; and I just had to. I just came to this point where I had to realize that it's more important that they like what they're doing, and aren't inhibited by it, than to cover one, two, three, four [topics] this week.

To this point, I have explored a symbiotic relation between the normalization discourses of the child and the teacher. "Learning by doing" and "scaling down" the curriculum are embedded in a set of discourses through which the construction of the child also constructs the teacher who administers and patrols the classroom. The particular "reasoning" classifies and differentiates the experience felt, the technologies applied to order teaching, and the "nature" of the child who inhabits the spaces of the school. This reasoning is not a formal, analytical way of thinking. It is formed through a grid of relations as different discourses overlie to give a location to the "normality" and "common sense" of the teacher.

TEACHER EDUCATION AS NORMALIZING DISCOURSES OF THE TEACHER

This section pursues the administrative and academic discourses deployed conceptually to order the planning of the teacher. In particular, I focus on the idea of the "good teacher." I return to the distinctions of hands-on teaching and the wisdom of the teacher's experiential (recipe) knowledge to consider them as not only confined to pedagogical discourses but also within ideas and methods that form the technologies of teacher education. I argue, for example, that the recipe knowledge is sanctioned at in-service meetings of teachers who are learning about teaching. But the distinctions about recipe knowledge and hands-on learning are also found in the instructional programs of teacher education as research about, for example, "the wisdom of practice" that inscribes the dichotomy of theory and practice.

Teach For America regional directors and local school administrators, for example, distinguished between theory and practice to give emphasis to hands-on learning. Value was given to training teachers through "doing." For example, an interview with a regional director focused on the belief that the use of traditional "teacher-centered" methods of teaching, such as lecturing in front of a room, was not functionally appropriate. The regional director, as well as many school administrators, praised approaches that were more group-oriented. "Good" teaching was viewed as the use of diverse methods and "activity"-oriented instruction.

In a different situation, a school administrator commented that one corps member, who won an award for her biology teaching, was exemplary because of her active, hands-on type of instruction. In her class, students learned about a variety of plant reproductive mechanisms defined in the textbook by studying different vegetables and fruits bought at the local store. A foreign language teacher in a different school was lauded for maintaining high involvement and small-group instruction in which there was a lot of activity. This included constructing a model town and labeling the different residential, business, and public buildings in the community in the language being studied. Little attention was paid to the content of the lesson. Attention was given to the process and procedures as determining the success and competence of the teacher.

The focus on process and activity as "practical knowledge" merges academic and administrative discourses in teaching. This merging of different discourses is evident in the idea that teaching needs to be responsive to different "learning styles." The problem of teacher education was to provide different strategies of teaching so that children could learn to be competent.

Educational psychology literature about teaching and multiculturalism was brought into the discourses of psychology that were previously discussed in relation to the pastoral care of the child. Educational psychology classifies "styles of learning" among children as either field independent—that is analytical, self-motivated, and the capability of working alone—or field dependent—that is nonanalytical, context-dependent, and teacher guided. Thus members of the latter group include people who do best when learning in cooperative groups, or people who have different cultural "interactional or communicative" styles (Nieto, 1992). In constructivist methods of teaching found in contemporary school reforms, distinctions are made between "constructed learners" (independent) and "authoritative learners" (dependent). While there is a recognition that such classifications can dichotomize and oversimplify, binaries are introduced that linguistically position the children in the schools in oppositional spaces (authoritative learners, field dependent).

This psychological knowledge about learning as field independent/dependent reinscribes the discourses of psychology and pastoral care into discussions of difference. The principles of managing "styles of learning" are to govern the soul. It is the inner dispositions, sensitivities, and capabilities of the child that is the site to be regulated.

But the field independent/dependent distinctions also manage the teacher who administers the child. While not made visible in the distinctions, the classification system is one that is historically mobilized for those who are classified and divided as different from the normal—the space inhabited by the urban and rural teacher and child. The discourses are made into principles to judge the performances of corps members. Here, in the "academic" literature, classifications of children as "different" join the practical and "theoretical," rather than separating the two. The academic distinctions between field dependent and field independent, and between interactional and communication styles among children, function simultaneously as knowledge about children and as knowledge about how to act toward children in the classroom.

In the examples, we can recognize that academic languages about the technologies of teaching are neither irrelevant nor nonpractical but inhabit the space that produces the urbanness and ruralness of the child. Through "hands-on" teaching/learning and "learning-styles," the teacher and the child are woven into and are part of the "practice of wisdom," the recipe knowledge, and the pastoral care of pedagogy—part of the grid that "makes" the teacher. The net effect of the different ideas is to obscure the normativities that intern and enclose the child.

A REASON OF PRACTICE AND THE NORMALIZING OF TEACHING

At this moment, we can ask: "How is it possible for the teacher to inhabit and to administer the space normalized for the urban and rural child?" One part of that answer is that the technologies of teaching separated the experiential knowledge of the teacher from its normalizing functions and did not recognize that the knowledge of practice is the effect of power. Thus, while we can say that Teach For America drew "the best, brightest, and most highly educated and privileged" from among college graduates into teaching, this selection process ignores the pedagogical principles generated for action and participation. While we can also say that the corps members in this study were intelligent, "caring," and "politically sensitive" to the social consequences of schooling, this caring and sensitivity were embedded in the system of reason that embodied a certain vision of the "reasonable" person who participates in schooling.

The scaffolding of discourses gives intelligibility to the acts of the teacher. The designation of "rural," "urban" or "inner-city" schools existed within an ensemble (scaffolding) of ideas about practical wisdom, the psychology of the child, and the populations that classify, intern, and enclose the child as different from the normal. The practice of wisdom and recipe knowledge simultaneously neutralize, naturalize, and normalize the social and political distinctions embedded in learning, achievement, and childhood. Although the discourse of learning is bound to a specific cultural and historical context, it is presented as if it were universal—or in other words, devoid of historical value and human mooring. The link between knowledge and methods, cognition and affect, is obscured in the practical technologies of the teacher.

My focusing on the scaffolding of discourses points to the fact that distinctions of teaching and teacher education have no essential meaning. Educational literatures, for example, continually treat discourses about classroom management as different from discourses about children's learning, as different from ideas about equity in instruction. We also find that such ideas as "learning is doing," the value given to the "wisdom of practice," and speaking of children as having intelligence and potential circulate in spaces other than those of urban and rural schooling. But these words and phrases of pedagogy assume a particular significance and definition within the space of urban and rural schools. The words are not as words in a dictionary but given meaning through the relations in which they are embedded as knowing, thinking, "seeing," and acting on the objects of schooling.

We can say, then, that the significance and implications of the discourses of teaching and teacher education are multiple, fluid, and contingent. Thus, while many teachers may talk about similar "things" such as classroom management, these terms do not stand outside of the spaces in which they are deployed. In the case of this study, the significance and implication of that scaffolding is the historically formed discourses about urbanness and ruralness of the teacher and the child.

In this chapter, by moving the discussion to the ideas and methods of teaching—the technologies of classroom practices—we are able to consider how the practical reasoning, hands-on learning, and scaled-down curriculum are inscribed in the normalized spaces of urban and rural schools but are not characteristics of practice that are in opposition to theory. Neither is the practical reasoning exclusively or even mainly bound to practice, in the sense of being "born" from experience. Rather it is a type of reasoning that normalize the ways the objects of schooling are constructed and acted on.

Further, the discourses about curriculum are more than articulating standards about learning. Organization of curriculum is re-visioned as related to the subjective, personal success and competence of the children. The bare-bones, scaled-down curriculum brings with it an assumption that there is some unspoken "base" of information and analytical skills that must be taught, and beyond which the curriculum cannot be further cut. To speak about, as the corps member did previously, the "few essential things I want to get through" relates the school curriculum knowledge to norms about the child who is to think, act, and feel as a competent "being." The scaling down positions the child, once again, as being "rescued." The rescued child is, in some way different from, even oppositional to, something that is "standard" and "essential" to another set of "normal" children.

The social space of the urban and rural teacher produces a moral order. The moral order establishes not only "the good" but also its opposite. The "practical" technologies of the teacher locate the child as a member of a population whose individual attributes and traits can be assessed and corrected according to normative standards. This process converts a mass of children into a collection of behavioral standards, norms of earnestness, personal hygiene, interpersonal conduct, speech patterns. In this way, moral traits are assigned to children. But the moral order is not only about the child but also about the subjectivities of teachers. The procedural concerns obscure the inscribed rules and standards whose consequence is to discipline the teacher who in turn visions and re-visions the child. The normalizations are so deeply embedded in the routines and practical wisdom of teaching as to make them invisible.

Chapter 5

ALCHEMY, IMAGINARY SCHOOL SUBJECTS, AND THE GOVERNING OF SPACE

In this chapter, I explore the alchemy of school subjects to consider further the scaffolding that constructs the "urban" and "rural" child. By alchemy, I mean a process through which disciplinary fields of mathematics, literature, art, and science are transformed into school subjects. This alchemy, I argue, involves a mixture of regulatory and instructional practices that takes place at three levels—first, in the content of the curriculum, which emphasizes the transmission of "bits" of information; second, in the emphasis that is placed on particular textual resources; and third in the tying of knowledge and subjectivities through testing and test preparation. The alchemy is embedded in teacher-constructed, district- and state-mandated tests that order the world for the "self." Drawing on the discussion in Chapter 1, the systems of reasoning about teaching, I argue, embody medieval rules about God in the secular classroom, and reflect a taxonomic propensity toward teaching school subjects.

For many readers, this emphasis on a "bits-oriented" curriculum, textbooks, and testing will not seem "new." These ideas relate to concepts of the "hidden curriculum" reported in curriculum studies since the 1970s. However, my interest is different from that literature. As in earlier chapters, I view the alchemy of school subjects as embodied in the scaffolding of discourses that organizes, differentiates, and normalizes the actions of teaching and children. The significance of the alchemy of school subjects, then, is not only that it presents an "official" knowledge through school textbooks and curriculum. The alchemy of subjects re-visions the social moorings of the knowledge as that of logical, hierarchical, and nontemporal "objects." Further, the formal texts of school subjects combine with other discursive practices to normalize and regulate children's productivity and competence.

The alchemy of school subjects is then also an alchemy of the child. An artificial order is created to distribute eligibility unevenly for participation and action—the schools of TFA are classified as containing children who are different from the unspoken norms.

THE BITS CURRICULUM AND THE MIND/BODY AS A SITE OF NORMALIZATION

The teaching of grammar, spelling, and mathematics, for example, can be understood as inscribing certain norms about individual competence and individual responsibility through the distinctions applied.

The discursive practices, as discussed in Chapter 4, involved a "scaling down" of the curriculum. Children were characterized as "lacking" or "having a limited fund of knowledge" on which to base learning. These discourses about the intellectual deficiencies of children were themselves related to discourses of school subjects that assumed a stability and consensus of knowledge. These discourses about the stability and beliefs about consensus of knowledge are not only of the teacher and of the school, but of curriculum theory itself (Popkewitz, 1976). The curriculum discourses and content selection of textbooks merge into a particular order of instruction, one I call "the bits curriculum." Earlier in Chapter 4, I discussed how the science and mathematics curriculum embodied a moral and cognitive structure to organize action. At this point, I want to return to that example to focus on the breaking of teaching "into very small bits" as a way of thinking about thinking and reason itself. The discursive focus was on "everything these kids to needs to be broken down so simple . . . [and] they need to emphasize those simple terms before they know what they are doing." Significantly, comparing curriculum knowledge to computer bits provided a way for the corps member to order the tasks of the lessons.

The idea of a linear, natural sequencing of the "bits" enables the practices of teaching to focus on the subjectivities of the child. When knowledge is considered to be stable and hierarchical, the purpose of schooling becomes to order and re-order how children think and reason. In an elementary school, for example, one corps member argued that learning grammar involves not only the acquisition of a particular skill, but also learning personal responsibility. The corps member suggested that when children learn grammar, the teacher's ability to control the classroom is improved. Thus, she observed that "[my] personal goals are to stress certain basic grammar skills that I've discovered the kids are lacking . . . to get them to take more of a sense of responsibility for their own performance."

Learning "grammar" is not only a way to master other skills of thinking and reasoning; it is also a structure that embodies rules of the "self" through which the child can learn self-discipline and responsibility. The organization of content participates with other discourses of the scaffolding to place "the self" in a moral order that is worked on and administered.

During an arithmetic lesson on subtraction with second graders, for example, discourses of achievement, competence, and salvation were joined. The students came up to an easel placed by the corps member's chair, and the corps member declared, "Okay, it's now time for us to do subtraction. Does anyone know another name for subtraction? . . . Andrew?" A student responded, "It's take-away." The corps member then delivered the following pair of messages: "Very good. Herbert [then looking at another child], Carl, get up and go to the corner." A child moved to the back corner of the room and the teacher continued asking whether the students remembered when they last used crayons to add. The students responded in unison, "Yeaaahh."

As the corps member stacked boxes of crayons vertically on her easel, she asked, "What's three crayons plus two crayons? How many crayons?" A student answered, "Four." The corps member corrected the student. Then she removed two of the five boxes of crayons and said, "Okay, there's five boxes of crayons. If I take away two boxes of crayons, how many will there be?" In a chorus the children called out "Three." The teacher repeated the answer while writing it on the chalkboard: "So, five take-away two is three." Then she said, "Let's try it again."

The arithmetic lesson had more to do with the discipline and self-discipline of children than with the formal subject of mathematics. As things were ordered in a regular manner, so were the children's expressions and body movements. The children learned to organize behaviors, posture, responses, sitting. The principles of instruction were about what children should know, and how they should "exhibit" success.

This embodiment of norms that join mind and body is repeated in a commonplace practice in elementary and middle schools: the teaching of spelling. In some of the elementary schools served by TFA, spelling was a central concern of the curriculum. That teaching followed a pattern that focused on words as discrete "things" whose learning had a particular routine and ritual. The pattern was pre-test/practice/post-test. These routines and rituals were found in a sixth-grade class where a teacher greeted her pupils by declaring:

Okay we're going to have our spelling tests. I'm going to say the word then say a sentence, then say the word again. No talking

during the test though. Number one is hedge. The hedge around
the house needs to be cut. Hedge.

The corps member continued, calling out such words as etching, cran-
berry, triad, blossom, hardship, dismal, darling, landscape, otherwise,
knowledge, spirit. This repeated a sequence of teaching spelling that has
been common in U.S. schooling for at least 50 years.

The teaching of spelling also occupied the instructional time in a
middle school. A corps member began a spelling lesson by instructing the
class to read the ditto sheet being handed out. The children were told to
spell each word correctly as they filled in the blanks on the sheet. When it
appeared that the students had finished, the teacher called on different
children to read the sentences aloud, and to spell the appropriate word.
This was to enable pupils to check their work. Chastity read first, then
Helena, then Germaine. The teacher said to Germaine, "Remember that
the 'c' in ancient is not an 'ss' sound, but a 'ch' sound." The teacher then
proceeded through the spelling list in this didactic manner.

The discursive practices of a spelling test are a ritual of learning and—
simultaneously—a technology of social regulation. The lesson is built
around a "text"—in many cases, a prescribed word list. The lesson is also
stylized with certain performances that children utter in response to a
command by the teacher. These utterances involve a bodily discipline as
the teacher constantly repeats words and sentences that pupils must repeat and master. Finally, in many cases, children are required to create
their own sentences with the "raw material" that is specified by the teacher,
and they are even required to mark their own tests, in the expectation
that such work will convey the received meanings of important words.
The organization of knowledge and participation creates an artificial sense
of order to knowledge and the procedures and processes by which such
knowledge is acquired.

In these examples, we begin to understand the alchemy of the school
subjects as normalizing the spaces that children inhabit. The teaching of
mathematics, language arts, and English is reformulated into pedagogical
languages that have certain formulaic qualities about what is "seen" and
believed, and about what children should "possess" and desire as normal
qualities. Knowledge is broken down into its smallest constitutive elements,
with the organization of the different bits into a hierarchy whose progres-
sion leads to understanding. The learning theory that emerges from this
practice is that the sum of the elements "makes" the whole—one learns
to spell words or bits of a sentence, then learns to write whole sentences
with proper punctuation, then stories, and only then learns to write
creatively.

While the bits curriculum dominates the ordering of things in the classroom, there are times when this curriculum seems less than central in constructing teaching. One corps member noted that while most of her teaching was related to the textbook, the content and manner of presentation of the textbook were not the only points of reference that she employed. Instead of following the textbook, she often "made" her own lessons—focusing on "things that I feel it's good for them to know." In her teaching, these things included tasks such as calculating interest, finding the volume of a cylinder, and finding averages. But even when this corps member seemed to reject the discrete ordering of knowledge in textbooks, her teaching still sanctioned knowledge as a collection of "things" and learning as the process of finding discrete answers to finite questions.

We could, at this point, think of the bits curriculum and the recipe knowledge discussed in Chapter 4 as different from the scaffolding of ideas discussed. They could be envisioned as built on a certain pragmatic model of schooling. This explanation would focus on the problem of management and control over children as a paramount concern in schooling. An argument that appeared frequently in interviews with corps members is that they are attempting to teach students who do not want to be there; students who often are not there; and, at a different level, a curriculum that has a tenuous hold in the schools in which they work. Furthermore, while the rhetorical pronouncements of schooling embody utilitarianism—students should learn now so that they will be able to get a better job or acquire some social mobility later—that sense of the future is perceived as having little relevance in the day-to-day life of students. Therefore adjustments and accommodations to the program are needed: "the bits" curriculum is one such adjustment. Using this argument, the bits curriculum would appear to be a logical response to issues of classroom management that are dominant in contemporary school discourses.

I have sought, however, to focus not on the intent of the actors in the school or the situational relations of teaching; rather my concern is how the subject of attention is brought into focus by the rules of "reason" that are brought into play. The focus is on the concrete discourses of management, pedagogy, and psychology as embodying a socially constructed "reason" to practice. In the discursive spaces of "urban" and "rural," this construction locates the children in an oppositional space—to use a phrase from earlier discussions, the children who "haven't been there." The problematic of the bits curriculum, then, involves not only an epistemology of school knowledge but also the construction of subjective boundaries about competence and capabilities. In this sense, we can think of the bits curriculum as a system of action as well as a system of reasoning.

TEXTBOOKS AND THE SCRUTINY OF CHILDREN

Within this system of ordering school subjects, the cataloging and ordering of knowledge has its tangible reference in the textbooks used to transmit the bits curriculum. Similarly, it has its reference in performances that are called forth through tests designed to document that the appropriate bits of knowledge have, indeed, been "learned." The use of the textbook should not be surprising, as it has been the center of schooling in Christian, Islamic, and Jewish schools since at least the Middle Ages. What is important here is not the fact that textbooks are used, for textbooks can play a variety of intellectual roles. At the turn of the century, textbooks referred to books written at the cutting-edge of knowledge in a field and giving priority to ambiguities and uncertainties rather than to prepackaged facts for children's learning. My concern here, then, is with the way the textbooks are positioned within a grid of discursive practices. In this way of looking at textbooks, my interest is less that textbooks drive lessons, or that textbooks contain stereotypes and biases. Rather, this inquiry places school textbooks within an amalgamation of discursive practices.

Texts and the Normalization of the Child

Textbooks organize a materiality through the rules and standards that differentiate children. The distinctions made in textbooks, however, go beyond the instructional level. The textbooks exist within a space of "urban" and "rural" schooling that is productive of dispositions, sensitivities, and awarenesses that sanction the child who is "teachable" or "unteachable."

We can explore the rules sanctioned as teachable or unteachable by looking at a high school mathematics class. The corps member teaching this class began by having students take out their textbooks and turn to a particular page. While they were complying with his request, he wrote a formula on the board and announced that the class would review for a test that was to take place on the following day. He then drew attention to the formula, saying that it is one that "we use over and over again to help us." "The formula is P over B equals R over 100. That is, percentage over base equals rate over 100." He noted that the book "calls this rate, rather than a percent." Then he showed the class how to solve the problem mechanically. At the end of the lesson, he admonished the class as follows: "Remember the formula. The book tries to trick you—to mess you up—because they phrase it differently. So, you have to be careful."

The textbook is "made" into a real thing that sets the pace, provides the criteria of learning, and defines the formulas by which one arrives at the truth. The text, the corps member implied, has intention; indeed, it can even "trick" the reader.

While regulatory principles are never totally coercive, certain moral codes are embodied in classroom discourses and performances in which textbooks are used. The management of textbook knowledge is also the management of children through the inscription of norms about thinking, feeling, and "understanding." Certain specific relationships between attributes of the curriculum and children's dispositions are revealed such as the oppositions established between the "math mode" and children's mode; science-as-nonverbal and English-as-verbal.

The textbook is a marker that orders children in the moral order of the school. The textbook stands as a monument of culture and educability against which children are compared and assigned to spaces. The textbook becomes a focal point to separate children according to binaries such as competence versus noncompetence, or achievement versus nonachievement. A corps member who was teaching in middle school described how difficult it was to work with children who were far behind "the expectations of the school." "I think a lot of them are still working on a fourth/fifth grade math level. That's sort of disheartening because these are supposed to be the gifted and talented kids."

The normalizing by grades that are explicit in textbooks, however, is not limited to the children, nor does it describe and circumscribe cognitive values only. The normalization is also psychological. The norm of student competence is also a value that makes teachers feel that they are being successful and competent in the classroom.

The combination of achievement and personal success was evident in the remarks of a Teach For America corps member who felt frustrated because she felt simultaneously constrained by and pressured to follow a textbook. Using it, she could "cover" the material, but she was unable to institute practices that integrated science, mathematics, and English.

> When I go over problems that do incorporate math, I . . . have to . . . grit my teeth because it's almost like throwing a wrench into the works, because for a lot of them, it's very hard . . . to get into a math mode. And when they hear math, they think, "Oh, math is hard." But it shouldn't be that way. It should be, "Math is easy; let's just get through it." It's the same thing with the verbal section, because I tried to emphasize the math approach to science, but a lot of people think "Well, science and math, they go together." But science and English are just totally different.

Efforts to institute curriculum integration embody not only norms governing the way each discipline should be taught, but also normative judgments about the child who must face the school subject. This second type of normativity is visible in statements implying that content "does not come easily to" the children. Statements previously mentioned, about "gritting" the teeth when talking about the "math mode" and the distinction between math/science and English, are more than conceptions about school subjects.

The discourses about school subjects referred to more than "merely" cognitive competence. School subjects embody moral codes that not only determine which acts are forbidden or permitted but also which behaviors have positive or negative values. The ways in which children pass materials, raise their hands to speak, and "repeat" in unison are disciplining practices that bring the subjectivities of children into focus. The pedagogical practices govern certain dispositions and sensitivities in students whom teachers monitor and scrutinize.

The School Text and Constituting the "Self"

Whereas in Chapter 3 I discussed how the discourses of pedagogy focus on the moral order inhabited by the child, in this chapter I consider the relation of curriculum knowledge to the divisions that produce the space of urbanness/ruralness. This entails a particular alchemy as the socially constructed qualities of science, social science, history, and literature are made to appear as a series of logical entities, or things of logic. In a variety of school subjects, disciplinary knowledge is assumed to take the form of a series of logical and natural structures that function as foundations from which learning is to occur. The concepts, generalizations, and principles of school subjects are treated as logical and analytical "things" to be learned.

The significance of this alchemy of curriculum is twofold as it relates to the scaffolding that I have been raising in this book. First, the social mooring of knowledge is removed from scrutiny. Second, the alchemy of school subjects makes possible the alchemy of the child. The treatment of school subjects as fixed and stable enables a shift of pedagogy to the subjectivities of the children who are to be saved. While the history of science and the social sciences continually point to struggles over the disciplinary knowledge as the focal point of scientific advancement, the site of struggle in pedagogy is different. It is a struggle over "the soul" to be redeemed. It is these consequences of the scaffolding that I now pursue.

The curriculum as comprised of things of logic establishes a vision of knowledge as a stable and neutral object that lies outside of social processes and social interests. This idea of knowledge as things of logic was expressed in the discussion about "note taking" in Chapter 3. Curricular "knowledge" is assumed to be in some way distinct from the individuals who come to school, even in current pedagogical reforms associated with a "constructivist" view of pedagogy (see Popkewitz, 1991, ch. 7). At the

same time, a certain norm is established about the sensitivities and dispositions of those who learn. The children who have the right dispositions
manage to learn and thus achieve redemption through their successes,
while those who lack these qualities become irredeemable.

Corps members are aware of some of the subtle problems that arise
when one relies on a textbook curriculum. These difficulties, however, are
constructed through particular discursive strategies. The relation of students to the textbooks draws on a populational reasoning that moves along
a continuum of normality/abnormality. For one corps member, the most
important difficulty of teaching was discursively constructed as being derived from the "low level" of student preparedness. Thus, the task of the
teacher is to accommodate to the students' special needs when teaching
from the text, and in preparing tests based on the text. A corps member
complained, for example, that only 10% of the high school population
could even read the science textbook. The practices of instruction combine reading with psychological exercises—reading the text combines with
relaxation exercises to maintain attention.

> The book is difficult. It's not appropriate for these kids. It talks
> about the properties of waves, but the students can't read it. . . .
> What I'll do today is review a little and break the hour so they can
> relax. Otherwise you can't keep their attention.

The book stood both as a monument to what should be done in school—
science—and as a reflection of a host of problems that arose when a teacher
was confronted with students who lacked the skills to perform at what was
assumed to be an "appropriate" level. Discursively, the problem was that
students did not have the skills necessary to read the textbook.

Again, we can understand the production of a subjectivity of the body
and mind as tied together. The difficulty of childhood was signaled by the
bodies of children who could not "keep their attention" and needed to learn
how to "relax."

The alchemy inscribed in the textbook represents something other
than a facet of the hidden curriculum that masks biases or stereotypes.
Instead, the alchemy forms part of a scaffolding of ideas that discursively
locates various children either inside or outside a set of supposedly universal categories delimiting acceptable and reasonable achievement.

Occasionally, the textbook revealed its importance by making other
"readings" possible. The prevailing relationship between knowledge,
power, and ethics is contested through one reading of the textbook. In one
instance, a corps member used a lesson about the arrival of the *Mayflower*
to discuss the implications of the diseases and disruptions that ravaged

many of the Indians who encountered European settlers and traders. This conversation prompted the students to examine some of the images of Thanksgiving that appear in textbooks—images that depict people sitting peaceably together. The corps member commented on this exchange as follows:

> In the beginning they were shocked, and they would never believe that anything in the book would be wrong. But now they're a little more into it. . . . [I had just planned for them] to do Thanksgiving Day skits, and they could have done the whole "friend thing," but they really were so entranced by this thought that they did a lot of skits of Pilgrims bringing "firewater" to the Indians, and not the "Oh, we-love-each-other-so-much-Happy-Thanksgiving." So that was pretty . . . I mean, they're very open minded, very accepting.

This reading of the textbook provided other possibilities with which to construct identities. It embraced a recognition of the social construction of knowledge. It inverted the official knowledge by making it problematic and explored other boundaries through which students could begin to think of the plurality of readings and possibilities.

Yet, while these rules of reason are contested, the search for alternatives is itself related to a scaffolding whose normalization constitutes the "self" in school. The efforts at "resistance" do stand within the field of unarticulated norms of acceptability/unacceptability, not outside those power relations. The bits curriculum and textbooks relate to the binaries and doublets, the "wisdom of practice," recipe-based knowledge, psychological individualization, and the alchemy of school subjects. The grid of discourses forms the reason of schooling and its "reasonable" people. Thus, while we saw isolated instances of counter-reading of textbooks, there were no systematic discursive practices from which to organize alternative principles of reading.

TESTING AS THE CENSORSHIP OF MEANING AND THE OBJECTIFICATION OF THE SUBJECT

Embodied in the discourses of school curriculum is evaluation. From stating objectives in lesson plans (discussed in Chapter 3) to the format of school texts and state-standardized achievement tests, there is the notion that formal evaluations are necessary to understand what the teacher does and what children learn. At one level, evaluation defines what is worthwhile to acquire and to master. It is employed by proponents of the cur-

rent reform movement as agent of change as different pedagogical strategies are sought to improve the quality of education. At a different level of
analysis, evaluation strategies are the effects of power. They incorporate a
censorship of meaning (Kvale, 1991). Although the English roots of the
word *testing* derive from a term that refers to an accurate weighing, Kvale
(1991, 1992) argues that in German there is a linguistic link between the
words *testing* and *censorship*. The test marks the boundaries of approved
knowledge and, at the same time, excludes any knowledge that has not
obtained official sanction.

The "power" of testing lies not in its telling what is cognitively achieved
or in its critiques about biases toward certain social groups. The power in
testing and evaluation is its disciplining effect. Testing links social norms
with personal identities through normalizing what constitutes an "average" performance as well as what constitutes the "optimum" level to which
students should aspire. By marking boundaries, testing objectifies the subject and makes him or her visible to scrutiny through the establishment
of methodologies for classifying the abilities, values, levels, and "nature"
of the child.

Regulating Knowledge and the Individual

Within the logic of teacher planning, effective test-taking strategies assume
a significance in teaching routines. Formal testing is tied to a system of
action for establishing the material that a teacher needs to review, for
objectifying the capabilities of students, and for deciding which material
should be taught next. Thus, the test-taking produces purpose and a "will
to know."

Corps members consistently "wanted" to ensure that students knew
the material that was covered by a test. In this way, they would be able to
know how to respond appropriately to questions that are intended to elicit
the material that has been learned. Toward the end of the first year, a corps
member projected changes in his teaching onto the second year. The most
important change, he thought, involved having a ready repertoire of materials prepared for teaching. Writing lesson plans and tests related the curriculum to the competence and achievement of the teacher.

> I would say . . . getting prepared and looking over the curriculum,
> since it is my first year teaching these courses; getting lesson plans
> together and preparing the tests; and all those things. By next year
> I'll have [these skills] from this year, but I have to get those pre-
> pared this year. I guess that would be my major emphasis right
> now.

But tying curriculum planning to testing involves more than assessment and preparation. Testing ties performances with students' thoughts and feeling in a manner that bestows identities. The ability to take tests effectively is closely linked to the normalization described earlier in discussions of teaching textbook and testing content. In the following lesson of mathematics, where students were asked to "think like mathematicians," the textbook assumed a certain nature that could "trick." Ironically, this concept of "thinking like mathematicians" focused on test-taking. A class lesson was organized by announcing that the class would take a test on the following Friday. The test regulated students through the content, time, and number of questions that were provided through the test. As a summary of the purpose for this exercise, the routines of preparing for a test were likened to the routines followed by "a real mathematician."

> You're going to have a test tomorrow at 8:08. Make sure you're on time. . . . You'll have 62 questions; they're not multiple choice. We have to work out the problems like real mathematicians. . . . You have to work on your own now. We want you to prepare for the test. Take time to study. . . . The test is taken right out of the review questions I want you to know. So study hard, use this period to get ready. Don't hesitate to ask questions. I don't want you to play cards.

Interestingly, although the teacher here was talking about working "like real mathematicians," the emphasis was on surveillance (test mastery and use of time) and a self-examination in which the students were expected to acquire the dispositions and capacity to concern themselves with their own conduct. Students were to organize their "time" and make sure that they were "on time." They were to "work on their own" rather than to be externally supervised. The ordering procedures of the lesson were outlined on the chalkboard to provide a sequence to the self-disciplining: Listed were specific sections of the textbook that this corps member's students were expected to review. He wrote on the board: "Vocabulary and notes (10.1); Acute and Obtuse Angles (10.2); Complementary and Supplementary Angles (10.3); Parallel and Perpendicular Lines and Vertical Angles (10.4); Triangles and Circles (10.5); Classifying Triangles (10.6); Squares, Square Roots . . . [and the] Pythagorean Theorem."

The discourses of testing also inscribe psychological registers related to the governing of the "soul." In addition to teaching their pupils the content that will be tested, corps members taught the performances associated with test-taking—a skill that is grounded in the ability to follow directions—and they taught their charges how to remain engaged by the topic at hand. The motivation and disposition of the students was the site of struggle—students were to be self-motivated and self-governed through "enjoying" the lessons and being "enthusiastic" and "engaged."

The pastoral power was not only that leveled at students, but the teacher's personal competence and sense of worth were also embodied in the test-taking. Even when students were unsuccessful on the test, one corps member felt good about her performance in terms of the pastoral role of the teacher—that is, the ensemble of techniques that helped students feel good about themselves and concern themselves with self-governing behavior. One corps member, when reflecting on the best lesson that she had taught, noted that her pupils had "bombed" when they were subsequently tested on the material. The corps member felt that the most important aspect of the lesson lay in the high involvement and responsiveness of her students during the lesson.

At the same time, the test attested to a disjuncture in the moral order inhabited by teacher and child. The mastery/nonmastery of the lesson presented itself as something that stuck in the teacher's head because of its pastoral qualities—but it had not stuck in her pupils' heads, as they did not master the content. Significantly, then, the test positioned the children outside the "reason" embodied in the legitimate knowledge of schooling but also the technologies of pastoral care governed the moral deportment of the child and teacher.

State Tests and the Sanctioning of Teachers

Although textbooks and testing-oriented curricula are in large part imposed by school districts to regulate teaching, the emphasis on testing and testable curricular material has been an integral part of national educational "reform," assuming new importance especially in the accountability movement that began in the 1970s. This movement encouraged the adoption of seemingly objective measures as the means to sort students by skill and accomplishment, and thereby replaced "subjective" measures, which were thought unreliable and often biased against certain groups, with measures that were billed as being more "objective" and "neutral." In response to concerns about international competitiveness, the current reform movement has reemphasized testing to measure the performance of schools.

Throughout the year, testing programs serve as an important horizon by which corps members judge their teaching practices and students' thinking. National standardized tests function as normative reference points. Thus, a high school teacher in California observed that "I still pretty much believe that my mission . . . is to produce literate—very literate—

students." However, when he elaborated on his most important goals for the year, he stated that he wanted "as many kids as possible [to] take the AP writing test and English test. . . . And I want to see them all get . . . at least a 'three.'" Standardized testing reinscribes populational reasoning into the distinctions of individual children. One corps member talked about expectations in the spring interview, and addressed the testing program in the city's schools. "I want to get them past that 49 percentile. I'm gonna try for 100. But I want them to pass the 49." A Los Angeles corps member went even further in responding to the perceived demands of testing. She indicated that the content of standardized tests was what defined reading, writing, and mathematics. This importance was determined by the fact that she had to prepare her students to take the California Test of Basic Skills (CTBS), which is given in June.

> My main goal is to make sure the kids can read and write and do arithmetic. Because that's basically what the state test is all about. . . . I teach them the skills that they need to know. . . . There's a time I take every day, and I teach them how to take that test.

Neither the task of getting students to the "49 percentile" nor reading and writing are neutral activities; they are built on norms and distinctions of populational reasoning and difference from norms of sameness.

The discourses of test-taking were not an anomalous distortion of practice among other teachers in the school districts; they circulated as part of the "reasoning" of teaching. Often, the discourses of school administration and "the wisdom of practice" sanctioned the use of particular standardized tests to structure classroom teaching. For example, one corps member placed in an urban area stated:

> My principal has told me that these [spring months] are the three months when the most educating occurs, so I am really going to try and make sure that happens. I also want to find out exactly what my children are going to be tested on when it comes to testing time in April, and [I want to] make sure that we have covered that.

The discourses of literacy and skills in testing inserted a universal notion of the educated subject—a "natural" state of being that seemed to make the way literacy is socially constructed appear unproblematic. Testing told of the children's normality and "reason." The tests also told of the social space that children inhabited as "literate" and "nonliterate" subjects.

To summarize, the discourses of measurement and testing are not "merely" about what children know or have learned. They are embodied in the scaffolding of ideas by which the "urban" and "rural" child is constructed. The discursive practices that define the bits curriculum/textbook/testing activities of schooling are related to the recipe knowledge, the wisdom of practice, and the psychological registers that construct oppositional spaces of reason and the "reasonable person." The construction of testing objectifies social and personal identities by using test scores to identify "self-understanding" and "intelligent" children. But as I considered in earlier chapters, certain sensitivities are sanctioned as the "reason" of learning while others lying outside the domain of "reason" and knowledge are omitted or censored. It is the sanctioned rules of knowledge that I tentatively discuss in the last two sections of this chapter.

THE THINGS OF LOGIC AND THE GOVERNING OF SPACE: THE MEDIEVAL RULES OF GOD IN THE SECULAR CLASSROOM

Through a process of alchemy, school subjects become "imaginary subjects" and "imaginary practices" (see Bernstein, 1992)." The formal curriculum of schooling reformulates disciplinary knowledge according to certain rules about school organization, school timetable, conceptions of childhood, and the psychology of the child. We saw the principles of reformulation in the patterns of practice related to bits curriculum, school textbooks, and testing. School textbooks make rhetorical links between what is done in schools and disciplinary fields outside of schooling. In this chapter, a high school mathematics teacher who told students that they should act like "mathematicians," talked to them about the importance of learning, and then proceeded to have them prepare for an examination through doing textbook exercises. These strategies were not an example of "bad" teaching, neither did they relate to any personal inadequacies on the part of the teacher. Instead, the significance of the alchemy was its inscription in a particular logic of practice through the scaffolding of ideas. We can think of part of this scaffolding as the making of knowledge as a thing of logic and of taxonomic thought.

Earlier in this chapter, I argued that school subjects are reformulated and conceptualized as things of logic. Privileging school subjects as "things of logic" introduces a particular style of reasoning into teaching. The emphasis in Teach For America schools on the bits curriculum and on textbook and test-oriented teaching accounts for a medieval cast that is evident in contemporary teaching. Specifically, in contemporary classrooms, the medieval assumption that there are ordained truths coexists—uneasily—with the modern belief that science and rationality will provide a better world.

Transcripts of interviews and observations continuously produced discursive practices that organized teaching as a practice that needed to "expose" students to new information and, thereby, "expand" their knowledge base in areas related to specific communication and analytical skills in written and spoken English and mathematics and science. Corps members simultaneously employed language that evoked a medieval reliance on canonical meanings in language to regulate the "soul." When corps members emphasize the "basics" they remind us of an age when there was general agreement among the "wisest" in society that certain kinds of information would best serve the individual and society—and God. Grammar and math facts are the modern counterparts of the canons that once governed intellectual and material endeavors. One uses these facts not only to learn how to investigate the environment, but to learn social responsibility and moral deportment by submitting to the discipline of education and to assume an identity.

The alchemy of school subjects introduces a taxonomic propensity to the reasoning of teaching. That propensity seems to offer teachers and pupils a well-ordered intellectual universe that was simply waiting for its proper "discovery," investigation, and expression. Significantly, the taxonomies that govern course content have their counterparts in the taxonomies that govern the behavior of pupils. Learning becomes the inscription of rules for language, information, and the daily practice through which one defines the "self" as a participating member. Taxonomies reflect the preeminent paradigm of medieval thinking, namely, the allegory.

The taxonomic inscriptions of learning are conveyed through the organization of classrooms. The chalkboard at the front of a classroom, for example, typically lists the sequence that will be followed in accomplishing the day's work: It enumerates the textbooks to be read, the pages to be discussed, and the tests to be taken. For example, in one eighth-grade classroom, the board "declared" what was due immediately (a spelling exercise), what would be worked on during the day (a grammar lesson on adverbs), and what would be required homework (a review of the spelling list, and an exercise in which students would identify adverbs and review the rules that apply to them). In other classrooms, the taxonomies that govern course content and pupil behavior are even more closely linked. For example, a chart that lists "homework superstars" was used in one classroom to reinforce the content-behavior linkage, since the teacher had placed stars next to the names of pupils who had completed individual homework assignments as required.

The visual space in many classrooms is dominated by reminders that educational life is governed by rules and classifications. Series of textbooks line the shelves, suggesting a batch processing of knowledge and children, which moves pupils through sequences, levels, and grades of information. When lists of "assertive discipline" rules appear on the walls of classrooms, they are complemented by lists of pupils who have failed to conform to the expectations of classroom discipline.

Again, this current categorization reflects medieval categorization of the "saved" and the "damned." This ordered space constructs and communicates the competence of individuals. The teacher—the center of attention at the front of the classroom—is the person who governs access to competence. The homework superstars—with their emblems of distinction—are those who are learning to be competent. And by the equally conspicuous absence of credit-signifying emblems, the remainder of the students are held up as examples of those who have failed to seek and acquire competence.

The alchemy of school subjects re-visions the complexities and contingencies of daily life as logical, hierarchical, and nontemporal, and without social mooring or historical embeddedness. The fixing of subjects is a fixing of subjectivities. The norms of the curriculum concern not only knowledge but also pedagogical rules that embody a continuum of values about the child's capability to learn such knowledge. Unscrutinized are the norms that differentiate children and make it possible to identify children who "lack" important qualities, or who have a "limited fund of knowledge" to learn what is prescribed in schooling.

SOME TENTATIVE CONCLUSIONS: SCAFFOLDING OF IDEAS AND THE CONSTRUCTION OF THE TEACHER

The organization of school knowledge seems to consist of sets of pragmatic responses. The concern with well-ordered knowledge and with specific bits of knowledge emphasizes a world of straightforward boundaries and explicit goals, and it undervalues the ideals that are associated with problem solving, discovery, or other notions of curriculum that have been conspicuous in reform writing on the restructured school. More particularly, however, the bits curriculum looks like a practical solution to the social problem of order and stability in the classroom. Thus, while the academic and social situations in which teachers find themselves are filled with uncertainty and misrecognitions, the curriculum, textbooks, and testing give a sense of order, hierarchy, and sequence to the organization and assessment of time in school.

Thus, the curriculum provides a sense of regulation and inner continuity in the world of schooling—a continuity that is not found if teachers focus on the socioeconomic circumstances that define students through categories of absenteeism, discipline, and achievement. In the "socio-academic" system of relations that teachers construct to segment knowl-edge for their pupils, the curriculum discourses establish reason and di-rection for the teacher's work when the expected acceptance of schooling by students is not present. The bits and textbooks, in effect, help teachers to control and find regularity in situations that seem to be precarious. Such instruction orders school knowledge and, through its application, classi-fies and orders students according to "academic" criteria.

But, as I stated earlier in this chapter, the seemingly pragmatic re-sponse is not "just" born from experience. It embodies systems of ideas that establish the distinctions, differentiations, and rules of comparison from which the "pragmatic" is constructed. The discursive rules construct a social space of urbanness and ruralness. This priority involves the rules of taxonomies, linearity, and hierarchy. The knowledge taught is a rem-nant of medieval times, when one learned grammar, dialectics, and rhetoric not only to train the mind but to master the rules of the mind, because those rules of the mind were also the rules of the world as given by God. All such rules emanated from the same place, and all were eternal.

Why is school alchemy significant? At this point, I want to signal issues that I will take up in the next and final chapter. The alchemy is embedded in a moral order through which identity and relations are established. That moral order treats knowledge as nothing more than a collection of things of logic and thus denies the role of moral codes in the construction of knowledge. Further, the rules for learning school subjects are regulatory as they involve governing systems for how one ought to constitute one-self as a moral subject of one's own actions. While learning concepts and information about science, social studies, and mathematics, students are engaging in problem-solving methods to inquire, organize, and understand what the world and "self" are like. Finally, the effect of this scaffolding involves a particular set of relations in the Teach For America schools as they are populated by various groupings of children officially placed into oppositional spaces that are classified as different: "inner-city," rural, and "troubled" communities.

Chapter 6

THE SPATIAL POLITICS OF KNOWLEDGE AND THE RACIALIZATION IN TEACHING

In 1932, the historian Carl Becker wrote an important analysis of the shift in philosophical thought between the 17th and 18th centuries. In his book, *The Heavenly City of the Eighteenth Century Philosophers*, Becker argued that 18th-century thinkers moved away from the idea of a knowledge that resided in God, toward a concept of a knowledge that resided in nature. This shift in focus did not involve changing the basic rules of knowledge. The rules themselves remained the same. However, these rules were now applied to a new location. Knowledge was moved from the heavenly city of God to the "heavenly" city of nature (which people then regarded as secular), where it could be applied to people.

The focus of this book is, in many ways, analogous to that of Becker's. For more than a century we have thought that we have been changing the rules of knowledge in order to make both schools and society more humane and more just. These rules involve an intellectual focus on what and who is represented in the curriculum. In more recent reforms, the search for a more equitable school and society has made the actors—who are privileged and who should be privileged in curriculum—a central focus of curriculum and teaching, such as contained in the idea of a curriculum that is multicultural. This approach to reform, which I called in Chapter 1 a sovereignty notion of power, has made certain gains in increasing the representation of socially, economically, and culturally marginalized groups. Yet, as this study has illustrated, the rules of representation and division in pedagogy have gone largely unchallenged in the everyday practices of schooling. So even though some aspects of schooling have been reformed, the rules of power remain the same as those of the past century.

Foucault (1979) has provided a way to think about the relation of knowledge and power through his concept of governmentality. It gives attention to how political rationalities are embodied in the norms by which we reason about the social administration of the particular modes of behavior and manners of "being" inscribed in the construction of subjectivities. In the instances of schooling, the administration of the "soul" of children is deeply embedded in the curricular reform movements. This administration of the soul gives focus to the teacher who is administratively concerned with re-visioning the dispositions and sensitivities of children. While governmentality is continually framed in terms of "humanitarian" languages about the productive citizen or a self-actualizing individuality, the discursive practices actually divide children according to particular values, abilities, levels of performance, and the "nature" of reasoning itself.

This division is critical in the discourses that produce the urbanness and ruralness of the teacher and the child. The scaffolding of the pedagogical discourses encloses and interns the child as the anthropological "other"—the urban and rural child as standing outside of reason and salvation. But the divisions and distinctions pertain not only to the schools studied, but to the reform programs that discuss the need to help, save, and rescue the child who is classified as outside the norm. Teach For America is a case or exemplar to provide entrance into the scaffolding of ideas that circulate within schools to qualify and disqualify children from participation.

This study departs from current literature when it seeks to understand the concrete strategies of pedagogy whose consequence is a racialized child and school. If I look at current literature on urban education, I find that it accepts race and ethnicity as the subject of policy and then proceeds to examine how identity is formed and inequality produced through access to resources and decisions. Heath and McLaughlin (1993), for example, begin their exploration of inner-city youth by asking about environments that "enable them to develop a sense of self, of empowerment, and of persistences" (p. 2). But while studying the narratives and activities of youth to understand dimensions of selfhood, the research accepts the subject positions produced through labels like *inner-city*, and thus reinscribes the very systems of normalization and divisions in which the urban/rural child is placed.

There are at least four ways that this study differs from past studies. First, it looks at the common-sense and everyday reasoning of pedagogy to understand how disparate discourses are overlaid to produce the space of the urban and rural child. Most educational policy and pedagogical research accept the spatial reasoning in its narratives of change. When one examines studies of race and urban education, one finds populational reasoning that is used to define the subjects of research rather than to consider how those subjects become objects of social administration. The reason by which urbanness and ruralness is constructed is assumed rather than investigated except in rare cases such as Tate's (1997) exploration of critical race theory and Gore's (1998) investigation of governmentality.

Second, the racial, ethnic, and gendered qualities of schooling are often assumed as fixed categories, and not as being produced through the spatial politics of pedagogy. Early in this study, for example, I argued that when the concrete discourses among corps members of different racial, gender, and ethnic groups were examined, it was found that similar discourses of teaching, psychology, and classroom management were deployed as systems of normalizing. This suggests that it is not enough to look at who is speaking, in terms of the ideological distinctions and racial differences of the speaker, without interrogating the normative distinctions of the discourses of change.

Third, through examining the scaffolding of discourses in the schools, I explored how the rules of classification and reason produce a continuum of values from which an oppositional space is constructed. To put this in another way, no matter how hard one tries to be average, the particular and historically mobilized discourses of pedagogy make it impossible for the children placed in the urban/rural space ever to be average.

Considering the problem of normalization enabled the study to move discussions of inclusion/exclusion from fixed categories of class and race, for example, to the production of differences that racialized the subjectivities of children. The ethnography focused on how the categories of pedagogy generate principles that order and divide the subjects of action. I argued that the "racialized" and "classified" space of the child is produced through the amalgamation of different sets of distinctions that construct an "urbanness" and "ruralness." The analysis gave attention to a complex, indeterminate structuring in a fluid and contingent field of practices that have asymmetrical relations. This structuring is about the dispositions, sensitivities, and capabilities of the child.

This is a significant finding when current research is examined. That research continually looks at the successful teacher in successful schools to find the paths for achievement, competence, and, I have argued, salvation. But the study points to how such research may actually reinscribe the very rules of the unequal field that educators sought to change. The problem of change is, I have argued, an issue of undermining the very systems of reason that intern and enclose the alternatives available.

Fourth, it is an accepted "truism" of liberal and left critical discourses of pedagogy that the site of struggle in schooling is "the soul" of the child. I have argued through this ethnography that this struggle is the effect of power that is played on an unequal playing field. Further, the challenge and resistance to this unequal playing field cannot be sought solely through focusing on who is represented, the sovereignty notion of power that directs most research and policy, but must be challenged through examining how principles of action and participation in the rules and standards of representation—Foucault's *governmentality*.

My approach in this chapter, then, is to bring this analysis of the spatial politics of pedagogy into a broader consideration of the discourses over which other, more consciously accessible, debates about school reform are layered. At one level, contemporary literature includes discussions about the need to develop a school that is responsive to its different populations—for a more inclusive, "successful" school, for a curriculum that respects cultural diversity, and for teachers who have positive attitudes toward and expectations about children from ethnic and minority groups other than their own. While the reforms draw attention to the inequities embodied in schooling, they leave unscrutinized the spatial politics embodied in pedagogy. The categorization of urban and rural schools as the "problem" reinscribes the administrative propensities of populational reasoning; the struggle for the sensitivities and dispositions of the teacher and the child "makes" the problem of reform the struggle to govern the soul. The spatial politics of constructing identities remains unscrutinized.

THE SCAFFOLDING OF IDEAS AND THE SPATIAL POLITICS OF SCHOOLING: A MORAL ORDER

I argued in Chapter 1 that the spatial politics of pedagogy can be understood initially as the construction of an imaginary "room" or space from which the child is "seen," talked about, and acted on. At least since the development of mass schooling, the school has connected the scope and aspirations of public powers with the personal and subjective capacities of individuals. Nineteenth-century mass schooling tied the new social welfare goals of the state to a particular form of scientific expertise that organized subjectivities. From contemporary conservative ideologies about a self-motivated, entrepreneurial individual, to Left convictions about "giving voice" and empowering the child to save society, the governing of and saving the soul through the construction of individuality persist in educational discourses (Popkewitz, 1996b). But the scaffolding that constructs a space of urbanness and ruralness is not only "imaginary"; it functions performatively. Principles are generated that qualify and disqualify children from action and participation.

One could respond at this point, "So, what is new? We live in a largely imaginary world constructed through our languages, and must live with that as a fact of our existence. What is important is to confront the racism of schooling and the inequalities that exist." The argument might continue that we have plenty on the plate of reform to counter the inequities of schooling. The "systematic school reform movement," for example, has identified multiple strategies for producing successful schools (Smith & O'Day, 1990). The problem is to provide a coherent educational policy that will enable the implementation of successful practices. At a different level, discussions of teaching and teacher education direct attention to the need for new forms of socialization as teachers deal with the demographic realities of American schools in which ethnic and "minority" populations have become more than 50% of the children in the country (with the irony of such a phrase as a stark reminder of how the term *minority* is a normalization and effect of power). The need is expressed for teachers to be more receptive to ideas of cultural diversity, and to have positive feelings toward and expectations of all children in schools.

These approaches to reform, among others, assume that power operates through the ways in which the actors (teachers, administrators, policymakers) feel and think about the actions of pedagogy. The focus on who is represented—the sovereignty idea of power—is important; however, it is not adequate by itself.

Such approaches leave the spatial politics of schooling unchallenged. We cannot accept the problem of reform as one of producing staff commitment to cultural diversity. We need to question the norms, distinctions, and differentiations by which commitments are shaped and fashioned. While traditions of psychological research might have us believe that the route to salvation is uncovering the prejudices and misconceptions of teachers and student teachers, such approaches ignore how discursive practices inscribe intent and purpose into the practices of teaching. We need to consider how intent and purpose are produced through the discourses that "make" possible what is said, "felt," and done, rather than as things applied to social action. While we might savor the idea of finding positive and successful teaching practices, notions of "success" are not free-floating, universal categories that exist outside the disciplining effects of pedagogy. Instead they are embedded within particular moral and social spaces patrolled by teachers.

If the range of current policy and research on school reform is examined, there is a continual focus on who is represented without interrogating the normative distinctions embodied in the discourses of change or "the soul" as the object of administration. When reformers argue that the demographic changes in U.S. society are a premise of school reform, such arguments about demography reinscribe populational reasoning to govern those who are categorized as the focus of the demographic counts. We can talk about multicultural curriculum as the representation of groups previously excluded; however, such discourses assume that the problem of reform is to refute the "errors" committed by past curricular efforts and to recover a new, final, unmitigated truth that is fair to all. Such approaches may change who is represented, but do not change the rules by which children are classified, represented, and normalized. When we approach the problem of reform as changing the feelings and expectations of teachers from negative to positive about the learning of ethnic and language-minority students, such reforms reinscribe the soul of the teacher as having the challenge of governing the school.

Ignoring the politics of knowledge at the level of what is regulated as reason and true/false is one of the major weaknesses of reform efforts. We need to shift the focus from the conventional notions of socialization of teachers to the systems of ideas embodied in the organization of teaching that construct and normalize the teacher who administers children. It is the rules that construct the social spaces in which we problematize the world and self that must be interrogated.

Foucault (1980) made this point in a conversation with a protester during the 1968 university student uprising in Paris. The student came to Foucault's office to talk to him about the new "people's courts" in which officials of the university were being tried by the people for their bourgeois "crimes." Foucault commented that although the courts in question were labeled "people's courts," the mere ideas of "court" and "trial" tied the resulting discourse into systems of reasoning and regulation that were themselves bourgeois. In this way, the construction of a "people's" court may change the cast of actors allowed to judge, but will leave the rules of judging unchanged. In fact, the rules of the court are reinserted as the technologies of "truth" and "discipline."

It was to understand the rules of "reason" that I focused on the scaffolding of discourses. The urbanness/ruralness of the teacher and the children is constructed through multiple sets of ideas that overlap and come together on a single (sometimes oblique) plane. I discussed in Chapter 2, for example, the insertion of social and political discourses about the urban and rural child as producing absences and presences (binaries and doublets) that defined the subjectivities of the child. Populational reasoning was also part of this grid that produced differences. In Chapter 3, I explored how the previous discourses interrelate with psychological discourses about the soul and pastoral care. The experiential discourse about the practical wisdom of the teacher and the technologies of classroom instruction was also part of the scaffolding that ordered and divided the child into the spaces of the "other." The amalgamation of discourses about the "child" and community; childhood and the "self"; "hands-on" teaching and "learning styles"; and the wisdom of the teacher's experiential (recipe) knowledge "made" the systems of normalization and division seem natural and unquestionable. These discourses are overlaid with the alchemy of school subjects that removes the social mooring of knowledge from school subjects. The alchemy of school subjects makes the alchemy of the teacher and child residing in an oppositional space seem reasonable and plausible.

Scaffolding is a practice that exists on a single plane. The urbanness/ruralness of the child and teacher is a recursive system of recognition and division that "tells" what is included and excluded, qualified and disqualified, from action and participation. That is, the different discourses in pedagogical practice "decree" not only the limits of "reason," but also the limits of who is included as reasonable and normal.

This attention to the scaffolding of discourses is, I think, an important aspect of this study. Most often, studies of pedagogy explore the logic of single sets of ideas, such as the psychologies of education or the logic of management techniques. When looked at as particular and distinct sets of ideas about schooling, the discourses of pedagogy might appear innocuous and even neutral practices by which teachers and administrators struggle to help, even rescue, the child. At a different level, research that focuses on the labels applied such as the "at-risk" child—in need of remediation—makes the categories in and of themselves the practice to be changed. The focus on the scaffolding of discourses enables us to consider that it is not the labels that include/exclude, but the systems of reasons that are inscribed in the way in which words differentiate, distinguish, and give intelligibility to the space inhabited by the urban and rural child and teacher.

Further, we need to recognize that the world produced through the scaffolding seems, in certain senses, to defy our sense of logic. Things that do not seem to fall together logically actually come together in practice. While we can talk of "things" that are first cast as negatives about the child, those things end up as positives from which systems of instruction are constructed for teaching, such as "hands-on" teaching or talk about children's potential that interns and encloses the child in an oppositional space. The contradictions and double movement of things enable us, like Bourdieu (1990), to recognize that the world is more complex and multilayered than what is described in logic.

Finally, my discussion of the discourses of urban and rural education as systems of inclusion/exclusion must be historicized in at least four different ways. First, we need to understand that the discourses of inclusion/exclusion are not fixed but have a certain fluidity as power is deployed. In different historical places, urban refers to identities that are urbane, cosmopolitan, sophisticated, and so on. The cities of the United States are enclaves of the poor, but they are also enclaves for the wealthy and the intelligentsia. One just needs to visit Harlem and the Upper East Side and Soho in New York City to understand the juxtaposition of different social and cultural spaces of the city. The notion of rural, as well, can evoke pastoral images of community and romanticized conceptions of a town hall democracy from which identities are inscribed.

But when the discourses about urban and rural education are evoked, they exist in a different social space. That space is one targeted for state administrative programs applied to ethnic, racial, and minority groups (phrases that inscribe the normalization of difference). The urban and rural are in opposition to what is deemed normal and reasonable.

Second, the construction of inclusion/exclusion involves different overlapping discourses in different historical settings. Once we leave the United States, the categories of urban and rural would not necessarily provide a vantage point to consider how groups and individuals are disqualified from participation. The city, in many European nations, for example, is much more an enclave of the wealthy, as the poor and minorities are placed in the suburbs. This difference is important as it requires that we have a historical specificity to our methods of research. While we can consider that pedagogy is a strategy of governing and entails a spatial politics of educational knowledge, the particular discourses and strategies of inclusion/exclusion are empirically different from place to place and from time to time.

Third, the distinctions of teaching and teacher education discussed in this study have a particular fluidity and contingency rather than essential meanings. We may find that terms like "learning is doing" and "classroom management," and speaking of children as having "intelligence" and "potential," circulate as terms of teaching in U.S. schools. But while many teachers may talk about similar "things," these terms do not stand outside of the scaffolding in which they are deployed and thus inhabit and are given definition within the different social spaces constructed in schooling (see, e.g., Popkewitz et al., 1982). In the case of this study, the significance and implications of words deployed are in the scaffolding historically formed to intern and enclose the child as something that is urban and rural and thus different.

Fourth, the seemingly natural impulse to rescue and save the teacher and child in current reforms is not natural; it is *the effect of power* that needs to be treated as problematic. The regulating is no longer to discipline people in an ordered time and space, but the enclosures and internments occur in a "society of control" (Deleuze, 1992). In the society of control, individuals live in a corporation of perpetual changing social forms where subjectivity is constructed through floating rates of exchange and markets set by standard currencies. In certain ways, the indeterminancies that Deleuze discusses as floating rates of exchange have particular sets of consequences in the construction of the urbanness and ruralness of the child.

There is a racialization that is not produced by being Black or rich, but is pragmatically constructed through the indeterminancies that make the child as subjectively different from the normal. These constructions, however, are inscribed in the reason of pedagogy that constructs the subject of the teacher's administration. The governing of *the soul* annuls the arbitrary divisions between the social, the educational, and the personal. The principles of inclusion/exclusion are inscribed in the "being" of the person rather than to the category of the person. "Instead of defining the individual by the work he is assigned to, it regards productive activity as the site of deployment of the person's personal skills" (Donzelot, 1991, p. 252).

THE PROBLEMATIC OF INCLUSION/EXCLUSION

The discussion of the spatial politics of urban and rural education enables us to consider reform strategies of inclusion as the effects of power. Traditionally, social policy and educational research focus on the problem of inclusion and exclusion through asking about the categories of groups that participate and do not participate in institutional life. Social planning aims to open spaces for social groups previously excluded in order that they participate more fully. This commitment to an inclusive society underlies U.S. reform strategies that range from school choice to efforts to broaden local, community decision making to the construction of national goals, such as the goal that "every child will come to school ready to learn." These educational policies target populational groups that have been excluded and seek strategies to provide a more equitable distribution of participation. The concept of power that underlies this view of inclusion/exclusion has been useful to challenge the exclusion of particular groups within society.

INCLUSION/EXCLUSION AS A SINGLE CONCEPT

While this study is sensitive to structural categories of inclusion or exclusion, I have sought to understand a different principle of power in the problem of inclusion/exclusion.[1] I make inclusion/exclusion as a single concept with different, mutually related poles. Whereas the previous notions made inclusion and exclusion as distinct concepts, the study enables us to focus on how the two terms embody the other. The single term of inclusion/exclusion functions as a doublet, each a counterpart of the other. Despite our best intentions, no principles are ever totally inclusive, but are instead based on principles of division and differentiation about who and what "belongs" (see, e.g., Popkewitz, 1996b; Wagner, 1994).

The doublet of inclusion/exclusion can be explored in thinking of discourses as producing "maps." As a road map shows us about distances and routes for travel, a linguistic map shows us symbolically how to order the objects of the world for scrutiny and practice. One such educational map is drawn through putting together the distinctions of learning, development, and childhood. These distinctions overlap in thinking about and ordering classroom practices; in the U.S., as illustrated in this study, they are often combined with other systems of ideas such as the child who is "urban" or of "the inner-city." The combination and overlapping of ideas function as a "map" through providing principles to reason about actions and paths taken in the school.

These discursive maps of the child are not only descriptive but normative. The map of the child who is *urban* and *rural* embodies distinctions and divisions to differentiate the children from those children who are *not* urban/rural. The norms that differentiate the child from others, as I argued, are not spoken about but are present in the discourse through the divisions that are made—the *urban/rural* distinction stands as a signifier of something that is absent but also present in the discourse. Questions of normalization are most often raised in discussions about the biases of intelligence testing. Less evident but just as important are the normalizations that occur as the territories of childhood, learning, and development are constructed to define and divide the successful from nonsuccessful achievements in schools.

It is in the differentiating and dividing of the discourses of education that we can reapproach the problem of inclusion and exclusion. Pedagogy functions as "maps" whose principles of knowledge circulate norms about the "healthy" child who, for example, has a problem-solving ability and high self-esteem. The norms about "health" and "development" appear as what is natural or universal to a productive childhood. But the norms of health and development are themselves doublets as they establish a continuum of norms that place some children as outside the range of proper norms of thinking, reasoning, and acting. The normal is not only what is average but what is to provide for progress and personal advancement.

The social and political significance of the systems of inclusion/exclusion is apparent when pedagogical knowledge is viewed as a strategy to order and divide children. Pedagogy makes particular sets of local norms as global, universal norms that establish the average. This book gave focus to how *urbanness* and *ruralness* constructed a particular normalized space or territory in which to locate the child as different from those global yet unspecified values. The qualities of *urban/rural* embody a historical overlay of multiple discourses that differentiate, distinguish and divide the child from "others." The division is unspoken but the normativity makes it impossible for either the teacher or child to become what is normalized as "the average."

The normalizations involve multiple sets of linkages. Notions of children's intelligence, potential, and growth and well-being are linked to other sets of ideas about "poor writers," "weaker students," and "student unpreparedness to read the school texts." The discursive relations embody unarticulated norms that, at one level, inscribe social and cultural norms of pathology into principles to order school teaching. At the same time, the doublets made the negativities into positivities such that the child could never be normal or average but would always lie outside normality. The consequence of the scaffolding was the production of a space that interned the child and the teacher as urban or rural.

Systems of inclusion/exclusion are also cast through an asymmetrical relation. Certain historical discourses are mobilized for talking about African-American children and Latino/a children. These discourses place these children outside of normality. African-American children's needs assume a certain unity based on populational reasoning, whereas the needs of "White" children are based on a notion of individualization. The normal is not examined, analyzed, or scrutinized, but is made to seem natural only when the non-normal is classified and defined.

The inclusion/exclusion also operated through the defining of absences/presences at the subjective level. The discourses of psychology and pastoral care, the social technology of teaching (its recipe knowledge), and the curriculum (the alchemy of school subjects) embody a normativity about knowledge/not-knowledge, successful/unsuccessful, and reasonable/unreasonable in schooling. The presences/absences classify what the child "lacks," but with the proper "nurturing" and the development of the proper "subjectivities," they can be turned into positive qualities. Classrooms are organized to bring forth something unrealized—that is, a capacity or a "potential" that is presumed to lie within the individual, but is not yet visible.

While this absence-as-presence seems counter to logic, the logic of practice is more complex than what we think of as logic itself. The absence-as-presence placed the child outside the space of the normal; the intelligence and potential spoken about could never be normal or average.

The asymmetry and divisions are contingent, indeterminate, and fluid. If we think back to how Latino/a and African-American children were compared, success (and failure) involved norms that wove together racialized, gendered, social class conceptions with those of participation and the technologies of teaching. The rural Spanish-language class discussed earlier, for example, involved an intersection of race, gender, and religion that was complex, multidimensional, and contingent. White male and female students positioned themselves as different from African-American female and male students. The exercise of tracing bodies evoked different styles of gendered and racialized forms of expression. The process of tracing each others' bodies on a sheet of paper evoked different responses and linguistic emphases that were embodied in the "learning" of Spanish. The different strategies for drawing and for talking about the body reflected different inscriptions about what was publicly permissible and not permissible—and what was racialized. The resulting identities had multiple boundaries and a fluidity that normalized and classified the children.

The alchemy of school subjects also produced systems of inclusion/exclusion. The alchemy produced an exclusion through removing the social mooring of knowledge. The knowledge of school subjects is assumed as a thing of logic. This also enables the production of discursive spaces of pedagogy that normalize the child through the focus on the social and psychological characteristics administered.

TEACHING AS
QUALIFYING/DISQUALIFYING PARTICIPATION

In this discussion of inclusion/exclusion, I have not discussed a broader issue of the social field in which the knowledge of schooling is produced and sanctioned to qualify and disqualify action and participation. Bourdieu's (1984) notions of "field" and habitus are helpful in making this link. Differences among people are, following Bourdieu, embodied in the habitus, the differential systems of recognition and distinction that divide and organize people's participation. For example, Bourdieu examines the distinctions that different groups have in tastes, such as what is eaten, bought for the home, worn as clothing, watched in the movies and on television, read, and so on. Bourdieu found homologies in the habitus among French primary teachers, secondary teachers, professionals, and engineers in how they "appreciated" art and organized their housing arrangements. These patterns of distinction and appreciation were different from, for example, those of office workers and small shop salespeople.

We can use this idea of field and habitus to consider the knowledge embodied in school curriculum and theories of learning. We can think of teaching as normalizing particular sets of distinctions and sensitivities that selectively represent the particular habitus of certain groups but are made to seem universal knowledge—theories of how all children learn, achieve, and develop cognitively and affectively. The theories of pedagogy seem to have no social mooring; this was made clear in the discussions of the experiential knowledge of the teacher as well as the alchemy of school subjects.

This universalizing of a particular habitus produces principles that include and exclude at the level of subjectivities. The category of "street-wise" discussed previously functions to locate intelligence in a set of norms that distinguish some generalized, unspoken norms about intelligence in opposition to "street-wise intelligence." The unspoken norms about intelligence function silently to assert certain universal dispositions and sensitivities to assess and compare different children. The definition of general intelligence does not seem to be socially produced, but rather appears as the natural embodiment of intelligence itself. Thus, the children in the class who are street-wise occupy a space in the field that is different from the embodied norms.

We can think of the systems of inclusion/exclusion as producing a moral order that excludes children who inhabit the spaces of urbanness and ruralness. The moral order is constructed through norms that distinguish, differentiate, and divide children. Moral codes are embodied in the ways students were asked to pass materials and to be recognized to speak in class, as well as how that speech was expressed. It is bound up in the testing that objectified the child who was judged and differentiated. It is embodied in the "wisdom of practice" that naturalizes the experiences of schooling and obscures the normalizations that position its subjects. The moral order relates to the alchemy of school subjects that stabilizes and fixes the information of curriculum. This stability enables an alchemy of the child who is classified through the rules that define the averages to be respected or the optimum toward which to move.

The spatial politics of pedagogy are ignored in contemporary research and reform programs. The moral order is both prior to, and a condition for, the transmission of competence in the practices of teaching.

To summarize, the spatial politics of schooling is the production of a moral order that includes and excludes. My focus on the scaffolding of ideas is not to argue against a curriculum that is more inclusive of groups represented. But I have been arguing that it is not sufficient to say that teachers need to believe in children as successful learners, that the school needs closer ties to the home, that the curriculum needs to be responsive to the diversity of the American population, or that schools need to be locally controlled—part of the mainstays of contemporary reform discussions. Neither is it adequate to say that schooling needs better recruitment of teachers, as was assumed in the construction of Teach For America. These tactics for educational reform are inadequate because they leave unscrutinized the scaffolding of pedagogical ideas that divide, order, and contain. They fail to look at the way in which the norms of achievement, competence, and salvation—assumed in reform practices—are the effects of power.

FROM AN ETHICAL TO A PSYCHOLOGICAL REGISTER

The discourses of schooling transform problems of defining and living a good life from an ethical to a psychological register. While there was ample evidence that the teachers, corps members, administrators, and Teach For America staff felt strongly that schooling should respond to social inequities, I argue that the concrete pedagogical tasks were functionally separated from the social commitments that organized teaching. The purposes of the pedagogical practices were not those articulated as normative purposes of schooling but the "purpose" inscribed through the distinctions, differentiations, and categories that divided and normalized the children in the urban and rural schools.

Central to this expression of purpose is pastoral care. The social administration of children places the ethical registers into those of governing students' "aptitudes" for work, moral inclinations, and the states of their bodies and minds as they participate in the social patterns of the classroom. Pastoral care, as I argued in earlier chapters, transforms "sins" that were previously monitored by priests into "sins" of the individual that must then be monitored in institutional contexts using discourses of psychology. Pastoral care is a form of productive power. The technologies of "knowing oneself," and of acts of "self-fulfillment" and "self-worth," involve the production of elaborate techniques by which teachers and children are both supervised and become supervisors.

The psychological register is so much a part of the doxa of pedagogy that it seems natural that teaching methods are processes of analyzing, differentiating, and comparing the "thoughts," "conceptions/misconceptions," "problem solving," and "learning" of children. In the case of the corps members, the technologies of pastoral care operated both as a moral discipline to determine what was just and fair and as a political technology to mobilize and utilize classroom practices that shape and fashion the "child." In the previous chapters, for example, I explored the way in which pastoral care was inscribed in the process of schooling through discourses of teaching that categorized teachers as "nurturers," "guides," "friends," and "role models." The strategies used to induce pleasure and trust in school take registers of social and ethical reflection and turn them into registers of psychological "wellbeing." Issues of racism, sexism, and multiculturalism are thus transformed into issues involving self-awareness, individual attitudes, and "beliefs."

In current educational discourse, children are "needy souls" who require "care" and must be "rescued" by turning them into autonomous and self-reasoning persons. The reforms embody the expectation that children in schools will be willing to express their innermost thoughts, attitudes, and feelings in order to find "satisfaction" and "self-fulfillment." Power and oppression are, in this way, transmuted into a need for self-inspection and self-rectification.

The discourse of pastoral care is in no way unique to Teach For America. It is a central feature of more general educational reforms. Contemporary teacher education reforms, for example, can be thought of as producing new technologies of pastoral care. The teacher is a professional biographer whose task is to change the acts of life to the reference points of schooling. If we look to contemporary reform in which teachers write "diaries" and portfolio assessments, such strategies are technologies that not only adapt the isolated individual to the social environment but also produce self-regulation by inscribing the individuals with rules that tie reflection to action. The "new" teacher is not only one who is competent but one who "cares" for children, who has a desire and an inclination to "know" the community and children's "backgrounds" and "needs" in order to develop children's "potentials."

What is significant about pastoral care in schools is not that it makes people self-regulating. Instead, pastoral care is significant because it creates a normative system that positions children on a map of individual differences. The geography excludes children through the division of individual differences in the sensitivities, dispositions, and awarenesses that define certain children as "others." In this way, the biographical and psychological characteristics of children serve to locate them within a system based on the classification of various types of achievement, competence, capacities, and dispositions toward reason or unreason.

At this point, one might counter the argument by saying that normalization and discipline are never fully accomplished. Arguing along these lines, one could point out that schooling from its very inception has never produced fully "normal" citizens. There are constant examples, this argument would suggest, of children who refuse to go to school, of girls educated in subservient roles who struggle against that role, of people who fight against the racism inscribed in their education, and of children taught about a consensual and harmonious world but who fight against the rules of that harmony by participating in environmental and peace struggles.

The difficulty of this line of argument is its reliance on a sovereign notion of power. It ignores the architecture that disciplines, interns, and encloses the individual. The purpose of schooling may not be to eliminate "illiteracy" or nonlearning, but instead to distinguish and distribute literacy by allowing some forms free rein while branding other forms inaccessible.

I can argue, as did Foucault in the case of prisons, that the school is not intended to eliminate social differentiations but instead to distinguish them, to create systems of classification for distinguishing among groups, and to use them to normalize power as transgressions are "assimilated into a general tactic of subjection" (Foucault, quoted in Dreyfus & Rabinow, 1983, p. 195).

NORMALIZATION AND POPULATIONAL REASONING

A central problematic in the "reason" of the teacher is populational reasoning. Populational characteristics are inscribed in the system of reasoning through which teachers identify particular moral attributes of children deemed to be in need of help. Populational reasoning does not appear as such, but appears within the confines of different discourses about teaching practice, school subjects, and the childhood of the child who comes to school. In this study, children were divided and grouped according to normative classificatory systems, which attributed particular values, abilities, levels of performance, and nature of reasoning to individuals, based on statistical portraits drawn of the groups they "belonged" to. The criteria by which children were classified and judged were based on "universal" norms drawn from concepts of "average" or "optimum" achievement levels.

Within these systems of equivalence, a new form of individuality operates at multiple layers for the child to administer his or her own self-betterment. Children are no longer "seen" as correlated with abstract norms about a responsible subject. Instead, populational reasoning individualizes the norms as though the norms exist internal to the child. This type of individualization is an architecture of regulation as it no longer seems socially constructed but a systematic "knowledge" about the norms in which the child develops "self-knowledge."

In this way, the notion of "populations" operates generally and specifically in the construction of individuality. The populational norm replaces the notion of individuals, who have personal characteristics, with that of groups, possessing generic traits based on statistical aggregates and averages. But these statistical portraits are brought into social interactions as they are revisioned as individual traits of children who are inherently "risky" or are dangerous to the stability of school and society because they come from a group that is too noisy, or that receives Title I services, or free lunches, or low test scores. Through the establishment of norms, populational reasoning places one's life on a specific continuum. Personhood itself is fragmented, and elements of it become signs of one's place in reference to a "norm" (Dumm, 1993, p. 189). Populational reasoning is so deeply inscribed in modern life that it is difficult to "see" without it. No action on the part of a child seems to fall outside the grid of normality/ abnormality constructed by populational reasoning. Statistically based figures are transformed into qualitative descriptors that can identify what is "wrong" with each child, and determine what must be "altered" in his or her "inner self."

THE TAKING OF A METHOD: A SOCIAL EPISTEMOLOGY AND THE RECOVERY OF THE SUBJECT

It might seem odd to some that a concluding chapter returns to a discussion of methodology. The rituals of science seem to detach the categories and procedures of a method from its intellectual organization. Methods seem to be technical rules that are internally bound to science itself. "Good" methods, the folk wisdom goes, enable us see the world directly—unencumbered by "biases" or "prejudices." The strategies used to define, organize, and interpret data, however, are political projects that "construct" objects even as they study them.[2] One of the major insights of postmodern and poststructural scholarship is the recognition that the politics of intellectual work is not limited to the ways that knowledge is used or in the strategic alliances that intellectuals make, as Gramsci (1971) suggests. The very acts of categorizing, distinguishing, and differentiating "data" are themselves political (see, e.g., Nelson, Mogill, & McCloskey, 1987).

With this in mind, I turn to a methodological issue about social epistemology raised in Chapter 1. My focus has been on the systems of recognition, division, and distinction by which teachers "see," conduct, and evaluate themselves as normal and "reasonable people." While I have used social epistemology as a theoretical framework to "orient" myself in relation to the field of empirical practice, I continually move back and forth between this "theoretical" problematic and the data. In fact, the notion of scaffolding that I utilize emerged during the data analysis as a theoretical response to the complexities of the data.

Furthermore, the method used in this study draws from a rethinking of theories of power, particularly the concept of sovereign power in educational studies. The method that places the systems of ideas (knowledge) about pedagogy at the center of the analysis has been used in other educational research (see, for example, Britzman, 1991; Walkerdine, 1988; Weis & Fine, 1993). This study differs from some others, however, in its examination of the scaffolding of ideas through which the teacher constructs the objects of schooling as well as the ways in which achievement, competence, and salvation are inscribed in that scaffolding. Furthermore, while I am sensitive to structural issues of race, class, and gender, that sensitivity requires, I believe, a consideration of the overlapping systems of governing knowledge that qualify and disqualify individuals for action and participation. The central focus of this work is, therefore, on the effects of power as it grows out of the historically inscribed "reasoning" of schooling. I thus focus on the politics of knowledge in comparing and differentiating subjectivities to understand the concrete strategies through which differences are produced.

To some, the strategy I have used in understanding the effects of power may seem to be based on a concept of a deterministic world that has no agency, and no resistance—in other words, a world that is antihumanist. More often than not, neo-Marxist analyses of schooling charge that there is no agency when the agent is not identified as an a priori condition of inquiry, or because words such as *resistance*, *agency*, and *contradiction* that draw on a Marxist–Hegelian logic about progress are not mentioned.

I would argue, contrary to this viewpoint, that looking at the presence of certain terms drawn from certain Marxism traditions as one's sole definition of "humanism" or "agency" produces a misreading (a solipsism) and a misrecognition of the problematic and problem of study. This study, like most current social and educational theories, assumes that we live in a socially constructed world in which reason is central to social change and thus maintains the humanistic focus of the Enlightenment. But the methodological strategy of this study is to change the problematic in which humanism is expressed—to consider the forms of reasoning through which we construct "the reasonable person" as an effect of power that obscures the human construction of our social and personal worlds. Such a strategy recognizes that ideas are material practices rather than epiphenomena to a "real" world.[3] The writing of this book, then, reintroduces a type of humanism into the study of education. However, that humanism does not require the definition of an a priori subject. Instead, it is by rendering reasoning susceptible to critique that agency can be reintroduced. This agency consists of dislodging the ordering principles that enable and disable action.

Thus, this study "moved aside" a number of conventional interpretations and practices of contestation in schools in order to focus on the scaffolding of ideas that intern and enclose the production of schooling. In accomplishing this task, I recognized that there are potentially different "motives" in the everyday world, as well as the possibility of counter discursive practices.[4] In this work, however, I have sought to understand the way in which ideas function to construct "motives" and "purpose" as teachers act to educate the urban and rural child.

TOWARD A RETHINKING OF THE PROBLEMATIC
OF INCLUSION/EXCLUSION

I have argued in this study that the problem of school change does not lie in identifying the successful teacher or successful pedagogical practice. Neither is it in identifying biases or hegemony within the official knowledge brought into schools. The focus on the repressive elements that prevent children from participating leaves unscrutinized the productive systems that generate competence, achievement, and salvation. These systems of exclusion are not overt, but are instead embodied in the discursive practices of schooling and reform that compare, differentiate, hierarchize, and divide at the level of subjectivities.

My concern with the scaffolding of ideas relates to Foucault's (1980) suggestion that we reverse the traditional belief that knowledge is power, and define power as embodied in the manner by which people produce knowledge and use that knowledge to intervene in social affairs.

Here we can return to our previous discussion about knowledge as recipes and about the "practice of wisdom." The production of instrumental reasoning is not "merely" a process of taking on given norms and goals, or of removing critical possibilities. The concept of knowledge as recipes, for example, is tied to various performances and discourses about schooling that embody multiple ways to define "reason" and the "reasonable person." The scaffolding of ideas is a normative technology. The teacher's "reasoning" entails a process of selective appropriation, relocation, and refocus that reorders the objects of schooling itself.

In this sense, we can understand intent and purpose as inscribed in the discursive practices of schooling through the linking of achievement, competence, and salvation. The production of the teacher involves reasoning drawn from several discources. Some of these discources are the use of populational reasoning as a base for political rationalities and pedagogical discourses; the use of psychology as a means of tying together the religious and administrative capacities of the teacher; and the use of discourses about childhood that position the children as being in need of "rescue" (see, e.g., Baker, 1998). This scaffolding is imperfect and sometimes fuzzy. It is pragmatically constituted within a variety of historical possibilities. However, it forms a historical trajectory that weaves together an "authorized" reasoning that frames, shapes, and fashions the possible ways in which we perceive reality.

The discursive practices of schooling are more than the mere transmission of ideas; the discursive practices constituted the principles of realities. Discourses are not just communicative strategies, but are also cultural and political practices. Furthermore, I sought to understand the way in which the discursive practices of teaching order and divide the world and the "self" in that world. These practices establish a moral order that places children into differentiated social spaces that function to intern and enclose them.

It is precisely the systems of telling "truth" and of "reasoning" about "our" world and "ourselves" that policymakers and researchers find most difficult to question. If we can play with a commonplace word drawn from educational discourse, the most important "achievements" of schooling may be to produce politically sanctioned ways of organizing, distinguishing, distributing, and disciplining transgressions through the regulation of the "soul."

This last point is important. The discursive principles of teacher education and teaching provide few analytical tools with which to "think" systematically about the production of power, knowledge, and subjectivities. Discussions about teachers' beliefs, about the wisdom of practice, and about the importance of teachers' "reflection" maintain a strong redemptive theme. However, these discussions usually lack the systematic analytical and historical tools with which to come to grips with the problem of the circulation of power.

I leave it to others to consider the ways in which an alternative set of rules can be considered. There is a growing and important literature in education (see Englund, 1994; Ladson-Billings & Tate, 1995; Wynters, 1992) as well as in philosophy and sociology of knowledge (Gilroy, 1993; Shapiro, 1997; Young, 1995) and feminism (Butler, 1993) that directs our attention to new forms of knowledge about the subject and differences. This literature responds to political issues about representation and the production of differences raised within this study.

But in saying that there is such a literature, it is important to recognize that there is no direct relationship between critique and reconstruction/development (Muller, in press). Each one calls for substantively different discourses, and operates under different conditions that enable and constrain its work. "Just as planning must be practical and strategic, so critique is only coherent when it undertakes a systematic interrogation of those constitutive grounds" (Muller, in press). The different registers within critical interpretive and strategic discourses should not be conflated. While critical and strategic discourses "live" in complementary ways and maintain "tensions" that produce certain overlaps, the two discourses have different rules of engagement, which should not be conflated into one.

Reformers and researchers have so "naturalized" the project of intellectual work that it seems only "common sense" for us to recognize the writers of reforms and research as bearers of social change. Too often we fail to recognize that inscribed within such strategies of redemption lie historically constructed power relations. There is no global progress inherent in the work of research and researchers. Furthermore, at a time when there is so much authority invested in scientific discourse and professional expertise and a narrowing of democratic processes, the privileging of researchers as part of a vanguard in producing change is dangerous.[5]

The role of a researcher is not to tell others what they have to do. Who gives researchers qua intellectuals that right? In examining the assumed "right" of the intellectual to tell the rest of society what to do, it is important to remember all the prophecies, promises, injunctions, and programs that intellectuals have managed to formulate over the last two centuries and whose effects we can now see. The work of researchers is not to shape others' political will. Instead, it is important for each intellectual, through the analyses that are carried out in the intellectual's own field, to question over and over again that which is postulated as self-evident, to disturb people's mental habits, to de-center the way they do and think things, to dissipate that which is familiar and accepted, to reexamine rules and institutions and on the basis of this reproblematization (in which he or she carries out a specific task as an intellectual) to participate in the formation of a political will (in which he or she has a role as citizen to play) (Foucault, 1988, p. 265).

Finally, to those who ask, "If reason is the effect of power, then what alternative systems of reason should be put in the place of the scaffolding described?" I respond that we must first problematize our knowledge and reason, that reconstruction is a pragmatic problem that emerges situationally and contingently through action, and that theory can help to point to "errors" but cannot provide answers to practice. This answer, however, is not that the intellectual resides outside of politics or outside the world of action. In fact it is just the opposite. I hope to have shown in this study that all intellectual work is inherently political through the ways in which it constructs its objects of study. Furthermore, it is a means of political intervention to disrupt the notions of reason that intern and enclose students. This destabilizing of reasoning potentially opens up the possibility of different ways of thinking, "seeing," and acting as we collectively struggle to make schooling a more just and equitable institution. It is here that the idea of resistance can be returned to but in different ways than posed in critical literature. In marking those instabilities we can potentially turn the weight of regulatory norms against themselves.

METHODOLOGY AS CONSTRUCTING DATA AND WRITING NARRATIVES

We can think of the more general genre of ethnographies as historically concerned with the codes to human conduct that order and give meanings to the "self." Even certain postmodern ethnographies accept this objectification of the self, but pose it as a phenomenological product of the hermeneutics of "voice" (see, e.g., Clifford, 1988; Karp & Lavine, 1990). My purpose in constructing this ethnography, as expressed throughout this book, is to understand how the self and the space of schooling are constituted. In one sense, my concern is an ethnography of the culture that we belong to in education.

At one level, this study followed the general canons of ethnographic research: the selection of schools and teachers, the collection of data, the organization of data for analysis and interpretation, and assurance of confidentiality and the protection of human subjects.[1] At a different and as significant a level, the study is theoretically driven. It is guided by what I have called a social epistemology that focuses on knowledge as a social practice (Popkewitz, 1991). Yet, while I approached this study through my own background in the methods of data collection and analysis in ethnography (see, e.g., Popkewitz & Tabachnick, 1981; Popkewitz et al., 1982), the research reversed the interpretative strategies of ethnography to make the familiar unfamiliar. That reversal shifted to the discursive practices of pedagogy that construct the subject and generate the principles of action and participation.

The "ethnographic" methods shifted attention from the groups of people brought into teaching through the recruitment strategies of Teach For America to the rules of "reasoning" in which the corps members were constructed as teachers. My use of ethnographic data of observations and interviews, then, has a certain unconventionality. I moved from the events, actions, and actors in the Teach For America to a consideration of how the objects in school are known, organized, acted on, and reflected about in schooling.

But to say that this study is "driven" through theoretical issues should not be construed to mean it is one-dimensional and deductive. The theoretical problematic of the study was continuously modified and brought back into interaction with the empirical data. There was a continual play back and forth between the problematic and the data collected.

Let me explore this briefly.

If I started with the procedures of data collection, I would discuss the field procedures of the Teach For America study in the following manner. Three graduate students and I visited different school districts in which the corps members were placed during the year. During at least three different times of the year, we visited a school district for a week. Approximately 70 corps members were observed teaching and interviewed in semi-structured approaches. Administrators and other teachers were also interviewed. The approaches were consistent with the methodological literatures in education and anthropology—in how data were recorded, interviews constructed, and data coded for subsequent analysis.

If I continued with the technical qualities of data collection (about 1000 pages of narrative descriptions), I would outline a sorting procedure that was needed to make the data manageable. The data, for example, were read and sets of themes or ideas (coding words) constructed to order the analysis and writing. About 100 categories were developed in this way—words to signify teachers' language about "school as management," perceptions of community and students, purposes of teaching, views about teaching practices, views about social context of schools, views about learning. A different level of categories distinguished the language practices according to who said what: corps members, Teach For America staff, teachers, and school administrators.

Some of the materials were coded in multiple ways: The phrases/descriptions about children and "self-esteem" might appear under categories about teaching physics as well as in distinctions about the children who were taught. This double, sometimes triple, coding is similar to Gregory Bateson's discussion of methodology in the appendix to *Naven* (1958), where he constructed a grid to illustrate how similar data can be interpreted through multiple theoretical lenses.

Technology became useful in the analysis. I started with a commercial program but found it was cumbersome when sorting the coded field notes. It took a lot of computer memory, was slow in sorting the material according to the coded words, and was not formatted according to the word-processing program. I finally switched to a sorting system that worked off our word-processing program. Its purpose was to pull up all the coded sections of the observations/interviews within a single file, such as all references to teaching mathematics or to African-American children. From these files, I could begin to examine the distinctions and construct a logic from the distinct elements of the study's narrative.

But in stating these procedural qualities, there is also a need to be more conscious about how conceptual and methodological strategies interrelate in the construction of research and knowledge (see, e.g., Danziger, 1990). At one level, the observational data have to respond to the theoretical interest in the study. This was difficult even though guidelines were drawn to direct classroom data collection. One graduate student, for example, wanted to give attention to the interactional processes that organized corps members' time. As a consequence, less attention was initially given to the categories and differentiations through which the teachers' practices were constructed. At the same time, the field notes did not distinguish between the actions of boys and girls, which meant that when the data were analyzed, I could not systematically analyze the field notes in relation to gendered issues as much as I might have preferred. I realized the lack of distinctions too late to correct as well as I would have liked for the final writing of this book.

I mention these events in data collection to recognize a complex relation. What is written as data relates to "theoretical" dispositions, which enable certain "things" to be explored and other "things" to be removed from scrutiny. One's observations place boundaries on what one can to interpret. Data collection and theory are bound.

We can "see" theory in what bits were selected as data. But we can also "see" theory in interaction with the data. The task of writing, for example, was to take the multiple categories of description and place them into a narrative that explored the nuances of power inscribed in pedagogical practices. This was arduous. I starting writing within some general categories that seemed important as I played and "interacted" theoretically with the empirical data. One such category was the psychology of teaching, which at various points formed sections of chapters and then eventually formed a chapter. Themes and subthemes were organized to describe and elaborate how psychology was inscribed in the discourses of the teacher.

The categories were not determined before data were collected, yet the categories were related to the theoretical outlook of the research study. For example, the ideas of student potential, street-wise intelligence, and hands-on learning became categories and then eventually linked to the idea of doublets. It was in the writing of the book that these categories were invented as I sought to make sense of the data.

The writing, then, analytically explored and wove the data into themes/subthemes that told the story of the teacher who administered the child. Here, we can understand how theory relates to data. Theory was constructed (reconstructed) through a continual interrogation of the data at hand.

The complexity of the construction of a research narrative is also part of the politics of writing. In the early drafts, I continually focused on the corps members "talking about" this aspect of teaching, or *their* thinking about *their* successes and failures. This particular organization of data gave reference to the corps members' intent and purpose in teaching. Through the structure of writing, the focus implied that the problem in teaching was that the corps members had not thought sufficiently about what they had done. The remedy, implied in the writing style, was that all that had to be done to reform teaching was to make teachers wiser. This was not my intent, although this notion of change was embodied in the writing.

A major task of the rewriting, then, was to redirect the narrative toward the "making" of the teacher rather than the teacher's "making" of teaching. Let me provide an example. A first draft focused on the sense of mission that the corps members had in teaching. The argument was how the practices of the first year changed that conception of mission. In the final version, the importance of the idea of mission was rethought. I placed it historically within a discourse of social engineering that had emerged in the late 19th century and was now being reconstituted as "rescuing" the inner-city and rural child from the evils of their community and their own "selves." By reenvisioning the data in this manner, I could think about the daily practices of the teacher as part of an amalgamation of practices that are historically sedimented in schooling as part of the common sense of teaching and school learning.

The rethinking of the interpretation played into the title of the study itself. The original title of the study was *Teach For America: The Privatization of Social Policy in Urban and Rural Education*. This version was a mixture of different stories about the reform program. At one level, it focused on the "children of Reagan," a phrase used ironically by a staff member to position herself within the political conservative landscape. The draft also focused on the different conceptions of pedagogy held by the students. But as I discussed earlier, these different foci repeated well-founded but well-worn sentiments about the inequalities of schooling and previous theoretical conclusions about the repressive elements of schooling.

Such an approach, I felt, was also ahistorical and, as I said before, recounted stories already told about the inequalities produced by schooling. This interpretive strategy took particular discursive practices of the political arena and inscribed them as the categories to fashion educational science. Privatization is an example of a political discourse made into one that explains and interprets the effects of social policy. To accept it as a category of investigation is to impose a circular reasoning. It takes others' definitions of the problems and solutions and uses them to interpret and explain what is known. This way of organizing the research, I believe, interns and inserts into research the assumptions and possibilities of political arenas that are being investigated. This inscription of assumptions can have drastic and negative results. A recent discussion in poverty research, for example, has pointed to how poverty research since the 1960s has used official state definitions to organize research (Haverman, 1987).

One can follow these changes in focus through the changes in the title of this work. The prospectus was titled *Teach For America: The Privatization of Social Policy in Urban and Rural Education*; I then changed it to *Constructing* and then *Normalizing Teachers in Teach For America: Constructing Urban and Rural Education*; the emphasis on the relation of identity and space through the title *The Spatial Politics of Educational Knowledge: Constituting the Urban and Rural Teacher*; and finally to *Struggling for the Soul: The Politics of Schooling and the Construction of the Teacher*.

One anecdote is in order here. When I was emphasizing "constructing the teacher," I placed emphasis on how the discourses that circulate within Teach For America produced its objects of scrutiny and observation—the child in inner-city schools. The selection of the final title was, in part, to emphasize the ways in which norms are produced to divide and differentiate children through the discursive patterns of pedagogy. But the selection of "constructing" also responded to a comment of a colleague who said, "Oh no, not another book on constructing." Such is the politics of differentiation with academics.

I recognize that my strategy of writing an ethnography is unconventional, in some sense, counterintuitive, and not without debate. But in the end, the worth of the research is not in its epistemological arguments but in the story that it tells to disrupt how we "tell the truth" about ourselves as teachers and children and thus open a potential space for alternative acts and alternative intentions that are not articulated through the available common senses.

NOTES

INTRODUCTION

1. I use the pronouns "I" and "my" here in a historical sense that while I am speaking, the ways in which I am talking about experience and reflection are also historical phenomena that make such talk possible. I explore these traditions in Popkewitz (1996a) and Popkewitz and Brennan (1997).

2. There are some examples of literature that push empirical/theoretical beyond the general framing of the sociology of curriculum of the 1970s; see, e.g., Gore, 1998; Ladwig, 1996; Walkerdine, 1988, 1990.

3. The chronologies of my "stories" would appear as: There are discourses of racism embodied in the structuring of the federal program to improve the education of American Indians (Popkewitz, 1976), the cultural and social differentiation produced in the reform program (Popkewitz, Tabachnick, & Wehlage, 1982), and the way instrumental rationalities of reform leave unchallenged the teaching assumptions and gender implications of teacher professionalization (Popkewitz & Lind, 1989).

4. The work of Michael Shapiro (1992) in political science, Judith Butler (1993) and Denise Riley (1988) in feminist philosophy, and Robert Young (1990, 1995) and Nikolas Rose (1989, 1996a) in sociology have helped me in thinking about this problem. Also, the Wednesday Group at the University of Wisconsin has over the past decade continually read across fields and introduced me to a range of scholarship that often remains invisible in the field of education. In this respect, the work of Henry Giroux (1992) and Peter McLaren (1994) are important in their engaging a range of disciplinary literature into conversations about education.

5. As I will return to this in the final chapter, my argument is not against social movements that mobilize for change. Rather, it is that there is a distinction between critical/interpretative discourses and strategic ones. The politics of conflating the two and not recognizing that this is happening is also part of the politics of intellectuals who wish to position themselves as authoritative agents in social change.

CHAPTER 1

1. Prior to the first Summer Institute of Teach For America, I was asked to do an outside evaluation of the program. The evaluation sought to understand

the practices and processes of the program as socialization. The notion of socialization in the evaluation, however, was different from conventional views. Rather than considering how students adopt or adapt to existing practices or how they negotiate meanings, we took a view of socialization as related to that of a political sociology of knowledge (see Popkewitz, 1991).

2. Numerous articles and editorials in *The New York Times*, news reports on the network news programs, a PBS special, as well as reports in *Newsweek, US News and World Report*, and *Forbes* magazine, provided a somewhat romanticized gloss to the efforts of TFA as its program formed and the first summer institute began.

3. The study was originally intended to take three years: two to be spent following the cohort of corps members and one for writing a report. The collection of data was terminated after the first year, but a second year was provided for writing. The interpretation in this book was sent to TFA for comments.

4. While I will discuss the discourses of pedagogy through which teaching was constructed, it is important to make a distinction here between how the discourses of pedagogy constructed "race" and the racial composition of the corps members. Approximately 29% of the corps members were people of color, including those who graduated from historically African-American institutions such as Howard University, Morehouse College, and Spellman College.

5. For example, one can compare the differences in the intellectual organization and themes in this book to an essay that I wrote as I initially began the data analysis to understand how theory is in a conversation with the empirical data; see Popkewitz (1995). The problematic of power and knowledge are in both, but its substantive development is different.

6. I use the singular "literature" but am referring to a diverse literature that falls under an irregular umbrella that I am calling "postmodern." Further, my interest in postmodern literatures is to understand recent theoretical contributions to the study of the politics of knowledge; it is not to celebrate something as "post" anything else.

7. The focus of group representation is important because there has been systematic exclusion of different groups of people in social, economic, and political arenas. At the same time, we must consider the systems of knowledge that generate principles for participation for two important reasons. First, the focus on who participates, while addressing certain categorical systems of exclusion, does not help us to understand the principles through which systems of inclusion and exclusion are generated. Second, as I will argue later, systems of exclusion occur through the inscriptions of dispositions and sensitivities toward action. It is at this level of governing that this study is concerned.

8. This does not preclude change, as Durkheim (1938/1977) skillfully explored when he talked about the introduction of questioning through the trivium of the medieval university.

9. My use of scaffolding is in a sociological sense of different sets of ideas coming together to construct the objects of the world and self. This usage is different from what is common in psychological literatures in education, which speak

of scaffolding as a use of and building on bottlenecks to develop adequate individual performances.

10. Ideologically, there were corps members of color and White corps members who spoke about the consequences of racism and poverty, although there was no intragroup unity. Some people of color spoke, for example, about returning to their community and "giving back" because of the advantages they had in going to Ivy League schools. Other corps members of color talked about growing up in the community where they taught and thus having insight into the difficulties that needed to be solved. Others spoke about rampant racism. Gay and lesbian corps members gave focus to issues of gender, but there was no single interpretive framing of the issues.

CHAPTER 2

1. I have randomly changed the particular location and the gender of the corps member to ensure anonymity and confidentiality throughout the discussion. The interpretation of Teach For America is not to consider the particular actions of individuals but to consider the ways in which the discursive practices of schooling were embedded in the program and how they function to guide and direct a particular construction of the teacher.

2. The disciplinary patterns of religion in the modern school tend to be obscured as "scientific discourses" reclassifying theologically related regulations of the "self." For discussion of this, see Bellah, 1968; Bercovitch, 1978; Kaestle, 1983; Popkewitz, 1984, 1991.

CHAPTER 3

1. The titles of these programs were changed to prevent identification of the specific school, although analogous words were chosen. For example, "Attainment" and "Crusade" maintain a missionary quality that was evident in the actual words deployed.

2. This analogy has important implications for the construction of gendered distinctions. See, e.g., Lloyd, 1984.

CHAPTER 6

1. It is important to recognize that the politics of inclusion should focus on what categories of people are present or absent in the official knowledge and public representations. But while this "structural" concern is important, it provides a partial, limited theory of power (see Popkewitz & Brennan, 1998). The concern in this book is to explore a complementary conception of power that focuses on

the effects of knowledge, that is, the practices of exclusion in the sense of identifying the principles that qualify and disqualify individuals for participation. Making knowledge the problematic of research is, in one sense, to give focus to how the subjects of our observations and attention are constructed as the effects of power.

2. I am not arguing that there are not "things" in the world—people do die of starvation; there is poverty; there are wars; and there are dominations and repressions. The latter sets of constructions, however, are things of the world whose material implications are culturally constructed and known, interpreted and acted on through the systems of ideas and practices applied. Research is world-making as well as a response to the things of the world (see Popkewitz, 1984; 1991).

3. Reason, however, is itself revised. It is seen as a pragmatic intervention in the world rather than as a search for universal principles about the world (see, e.g., Cherryholmes, 1988; Rorty, 1989).

4. My argument is not that I have found the new millennium through a focus on knowledge/power relations; I recognize a need for historical scrutiny of my own discursive practices. Further, I recognize that my tactics of study need to be continually confronted through challenging their own tendencies and recognizing there are no ultimate, foundational notions of progress or essential methods of study.

5. I discuss these issues in Popkewitz, 1991, 1996a.

APPENDIX

1. The focus on knowledge rather than on individuals makes this issue of confidentiality less prominent.

REFERENCES

Appiah, K. (1992). *In my father's house: Africa in the philosophy of culture.* New York: Oxford University Press.

Baker, B. (1998). Childhood-as-rescue in the emergence and spread of the U.S. public school. In T. Popkewitz & M. Brennan (Eds.), *Foucault's challenge: Discourse, knowledge, and power in education* (pp. 117–143). New York: Teachers College Press.

Bateson, G. (1958). *The Naven: A survey of the problems suggested by a compositive picture of the culture of a New Guinea tribe drawn from three points of view.* Stanford: Stanford University Press.

Becker, C. (1932). *The heavenly city of the eighteenth-century philosophers.* New Haven: Yale University Press.

Bellah, R. (1968). Civil religion in America. In W. McLoughlin & R. Bellah (Eds.), *Religion in America* (pp. 3–23). Boston: Houghton Mifflin Company.

Bercovitch, S. (1978). *The American Jeremiad.* Madison: University of Wisconsin Press.

Berger, P., & Luckmann, T. (1967). *The social construction of reality: A treatise in the sociology of knowledge.* Garden City, NY: Anchor.

Bernstein, B. (1992). *The structuring of pedagogical discourse: Class, codes and control* (Vol. 4). New York: Routledge.

Bourdieu, P. (1984). *Distinction: A social critique of the judgment of taste.* Cambridge: Harvard University Press.

Bourdieu, P. (1990). *The logic of practice.* Stanford: Stanford University Press.

Bourdieu, P. (1991). *Language and symbolic power* (J. Thompson, Ed.; M. Adamson, Trans.). Cambridge: Harvard University Press.

Bourdieu, P., & Wacquant, L. (1992). *An invitation to reflexive sociology.* Chicago: University of Chicago Press.

Britzman, D. (1991). *Practice makes practice: A critical study of learning to teach.* Albany: State University of New York Press.

Bruckerhoff, C. (1991). *Between classes: Faculty life at Truman High.* New York: Teachers College Press.

Butler, J. (1992). Contingent foundations: Feminism and the question of "postmodernism." In J. Butler & J. Scott (Eds.), *Feminists theorize the political* (pp. 3–21). New York: Routledge.

Butler, J. (1993). *Bodies that matter: On the discourse limits of "sex."* New York: Routledge.

Carr, W., & Kemmis, S. (1986). *Becoming critical: Education, knowledge and action research.* New York: Falmer Press.

Castel, R. (1991). From dangerousness to risk. In G. Burchell, C. Gordon, & P. Miller (Eds.), *The Foucault effect: Studies in governmentality* (pp. 281–298). Chicago: University of Chicago Press.

Cherryholmes, C. (1988). *Power and criticism: Poststructural investigations in education.* New York: Teachers College Press.

Clifford, J. (1988). *The predicament of culture: Twentieth-century ethnography, literature, and art.* Cambridge: Harvard University Press.

Danziger, K. (1990). *Constructing the subject: Historical origins of psychological research.* New York: Cambridge University Press.

Deleuze, G. (1992). Postscript on the societies of control. *October, 59 (Winter),* 3–7.

Delpit, L. (1988). The silenced dialogue: Power and pedagogy in educating other people's children. *Harvard Educational Review, 58,* 280–298.

Donzelot, J. (1991). Pleasure in work. In G. Burchell, C. Gordon, & P. Miller (Eds.), *The Foucault effect: Studies in governmentality* (pp. 251–280). Chicago: University of Chicago Press.

Dreyfus, H., & Rabinow, P. (1983). *Michel Foucault: Beyond structuralism and hermeneutics.* Chicago: University of Chicago Press.

Dumm, T. (1987). *Democracy and punishment: Disciplinary origins of the United States.* Madison: University of Wisconsin Press.

Dumm, T. (1993). The new enclosures: Racism in the normalized community. In R. Gooding-Williams (Ed.), *Reading Rodney King: Reading urban uprising* (pp. 178–195). New York: Routledge.

Durkheim, E. (1977). *The evolution of educational thought: Lectures on the formation and development of secondary education in France* (P. Collins, Trans.). London: Routledge, Kegan & Paul. (Original work published, 1938)

Englund, T. (1994). Education as a citizenship right—a concept in transition: Sweden related to other Western democracies and political philosophy. *Curriculum Studies, 26,* 383–399.

Fendler, L. (1998). What is it impossible to think? A genealogy of the educated subject. In T. Popkewitz & M. Brennan (Eds.), *Foucault's challenge: Discourse, knowledge, and power in education* (pp. 39–63). New York: Teachers College Press.

Foucault, M. (1979). Governmentality. *Ideology and Consciousness, 6,* 5–22.

Foucault, M. (1980). *Power/knowledge: Selected interviews and other writings by Michel Foucault, 1972–1977* (C. Gordon, Trans. & Ed.). New York: Pantheon.

Foucault, M. (1988). The political technology of individuals. In L. Martin, H. Gutman, & P. Huttan (Eds.), *Technologies of the self* (pp. 145–162). Amherst: University of Massachusetts Press.

Gilroy, P. (1993). *The Black Atlantic: Modernity and double consciousness.* Cambridge: Harvard University.

Giroux, H. (1992). *Border crossings: Cultural workers and the politics of education.* New York: Routledge.

Gore, J. (1992). *The struggles for pedagogies.* New York: Routledge.

Gore, J. (1998). Disciplining bodies: On the continuity of power relations in pedagogy. In T. Popkewitz & M. Brennan (Eds.), *Foucault's challenge: Discourse, knowledge, and power in education* (pp. 231–254). New York: Teachers College Press.

Gramsci, A. (1971). *Sections from the prison notebooks of Antonio Gramsci* (Q. Hoare & G. Nowell Smith, Trans.). New York: International Publishers.

Graue, M. (1993). *Ready for what? Constructing meaning of readiness for kindergarten.* Albany: State University of New York Press.

Hacking, I. (1990). *The taming of chance.* New York: Cambridge University Press.

Hacking, I. (1991). How should we do the history of statistics? In G. Burchell, C. Gordon, & P. Miller (Eds.), *The Foucault effect: Studies in governmentality* (pp. 181–196). Chicago: University of Chicago Press.

Haveman, R. (1987). *Poverty policy and poverty research: The great society and the social sciences.* Madison: University of Wisconsin Press.

Heath, S. B., & McLaughlin, M. (Eds.). (1993). *Identity and inner-city youth. Beyond ethnicity and gender.* New York: Teachers College Press.

Hennon, L. (in press). The construction of discursive space as patterns of inclusion/exclusion: Governmentality and urbanism in the USA. In T. Popkewitz (Ed.), *Educational knowledge: Changing relationships between the state, civil society, and the educational community.* Albany, NY: The State University of New York.

Hunter, I. (1994). *Rethinking the school: Subjectivity, bureaucracy, criticism.* New York: St. Martin's Press.

Kaestle, C. (1983). *Pillars of the republic: Common schools and American society, 1780–1860.* New York: Hill and Wang.

Karp, I., & Lavine, S. (1990). *Exhibiting cultures: The poetics and politics of museum display.* Washington, D.C.: Smithsonian Institution Press.

Kuhn, T. (1970). *The structure of scientific revolutions* (2nd ed.). Chicago: University of Chicago Press.

Kvale, S. (1991). Evaluation and decentralization of knowledge. In M. Granheim, M. Kogan, & U. Lundgren (Eds.), *Evaluation as policymaking; Introducing evaluation into a national decentralized educational system* (pp. 119–140). London: Jessica Kingsley.

Kvale, S. (Ed.). (1992). *Psychology and postmodernism.* London: Sage Publications.

Ladson-Billings, G., & Tate, B. (1995). Toward a critical race theory of education. *Teachers College Record, 97,* 47–68.

Ladwig, J. (1996). *Academic distinctions; Theory and methodology in the sociology of school/knowledge.* New York: Routledge.

Leys, R. (1994). Mead's voice: Imitation as foundation; or, the struggle against mimesis. In D. Ross (Ed.), *Modernist impulses in the human sciences 1870–1930* (pp. 320–235). Baltimore: Johns Hopkins University Press.

Lloyd, G. (1984). *The man of reason: "Male" and "female" in Western philosophy.* Minneapolis: University of Minnesota Press.

Marx, L. (1964). *The machine in the garden: Technology and the pastoral image in America.* New York: Oxford University Press.

Mattingly, P. (1975). *The classless profession: American schoolmen in the nineteenth century.* New York: New York University Press.

McCarthy, C., & Crichlow, W. (Eds.). (1993). *Race, identity and representation in education.* New York: Routledge.

McLaren, P. (1994). *Schooling as a ritual performance* (2nd ed.). Boston: Routledge & Kegan Paul.

McNeil, L. (1986). *Contradictions of control: School structure and school knowledge.* London & New York: Routledge & Kegan Paul.

Morrison, T. (1992). *Playing in the dark: Whiteness and the literary imagination.* Cambridge: Harvard University Press.

Muller, J. (in press). Critics and reconstructors: On the emergence of progressive educational expertise in South Africa. In T. Popkewitz & A. Kazamias (Eds.), *Educational knowledge: Changing relationships between the state, civil society, and the educational community.* Albany: State University of New York Press.

National Commission on Excellence in Education. (1983). A Nation-At-Risk: The Imperative of Educational Reform. U.S. Government Printing Office: Washington, D.C.

Nelson, J., Mogill, A., & McCloskey, D. (Eds.). (1987). *The rhetoric of the human sciences.* Madison: University of Wisconsin Press.

Nieto, S. (1992). *Affirming diversity: The sociopolitical context of multicultural education.* New York: Longman.

O'Donnell, J. (1985). *The origins of behaviorism: American psychology, 1876–1920.* New York: New York University Press.

Page, R. (1991). *Lower-tract classrooms: A curricular and cultural perspective.* New York: Teachers College Press.

Popkewitz, T. (1976). Reform as political discourse: A case study. *School Review, 84,* 43–69.

Popkewitz, T. (1984). *Paradigm and ideology in educational research: Social functions of the intellectual.* London & New York: Falmer Press.

Popkewitz, T. (1991). *A political sociology of educational reform: Power/knowledge in teaching, teacher education, and research.* New York: Teachers College Press.

Popkewitz, T. (1995). Policy, knowledge and power: Some issues for the study of educational reform. In P. Cookson & B. Schneider (Eds.), *Transforming schools: Trends, dilemmas and prospects* (pp. 413–457). New York: Garland Press.

Popkewitz, T. (1996a). Critical tradition and its linguistic turn. In P. Higgs (Ed.), *Metatheories in philosophy of education.* Durban, S.A.: Heinemann.

Popkewitz, T. (1996b). Rethinking decentralization and state/civil society distinctions: The state of a problematic of governing. *Journal of Educational Policy, 11*(1), 27–51.

Popkewitz, T. (in press). The administration of freedom and the redemptive discourses of the educational sciences. *Review of Educational Research.*

Popkewitz, T., & Brennan, M. (1998). Restructuring of social and political theory: Foucault and a social epistemology of school practices. *Educational Theory, 47/3,* 287–314.

Popkewitz, T., & Lind, K. (1989). Teacher incentives as reform: Implications for teachers' work and the changing control mechanism in education. *Teachers College Record, 90,* 575–594.

Popkewitz, T., & Tabachnick, B. R. (Eds.). (1981). *The study of schooling: Field methodology in educational research.* New York: Praeger.

Popkewitz, T., Tabachnick, B., & Wehlage, G. (1982). *The myth of educational reform: A study of school responses to a program of change.* Madison: University of Wisconsin Press.

Romberg, T., Zarinia, E., & Williams, S. (1989). Mandated school mathematics testing in the United States: A survey of state mathematics supervisors. Madison: The Wisconsin Center for Educational Research.

Riley, D. (1988). *Am I that name? Feminism and the category of "women" in history.* Minneapolis: University of Minnesota Press.

Rorty, R. (1989). *Contingency, irony and solidarity.* New York: Cambridge University Press.

Rose, N. (1989). *Governing the soul.* New York: Routledge, Chapman & Hall.

Rose, N. (1996a). The death of the social? Re-figuring the territory of government. *Economy and Society, 25,* 327–356.

Rose, N. (1996b). *Inventing ourselves; Psychology, power, and personhood.* New York: Cambridge University Press.

Rose, N., & Miller, P. (1992). Political power beyond the state: Problematics of government. *British Journal of Sociology, 43,* 173–205.

Scott, J. (1990). *Domination and the arts of resistance: Hidden transcripts.* New Haven: Yale University Press.

Sennett, R. (1994). *Flesh and stone: The body and the city in western civilization.* New York and London: W.W. Norton & Company.

Shapiro, M. (1992). *Reading the postmodern polity: Political theory as textual practice.* Minneapolis: University of Minnesota Press.

Shapiro, M. (1997). *Violent cartographies: Mapping the culture of war.* Minneapolis: University of Minnesota Press.

Sleeter, C., & Grant, C. (1994). *Making choices for multicultural education: Five approaches to race, class, and gender* (2nd ed.). New York: Merrill.

Smith, M., & O'Day, J. (1990). Systemic school reform. *Politics of Education Association Yearbook,* 233–267.

Tate, W. (1997). Critical race theory and education: History, theory, and implications. In M. Apple (Ed.), *Review of research in education* (Vol. 22, pp. 195–250). Washington, D.C.: American Educational Research Association.

Tate, W., Ladson-Billings, G., & Grant, C. (1993). The Brown decision revised: Mathematizing social problems. *Educational Policy, 7,* 255–275.

Teach For America. (n.d.). *Institute Summary.* Unpublished manuscript. New York: Author.

Wagner, P. (1994). *The sociology of modernity.* New York: Routledge.

Walkerdine, V. (1988). *The mastery of reason: Cognitive development and the production of rationality.* London: Routledge.

Walkerdine, V. (1990). *School girl fictions.* London: Verso.

Weis, L., & Fine, M. (Eds.). (1993). *Beyond silenced voices: Class, race, and gender in United States schools*. Albany: State University of New York.

Wynters, S. (1992*). Do not call us "negros:" How multicultural textbooks perpetuate racism*. San Francisco: Aspire Books.

Young, M. (Ed.). (1971). *Knowledge and control; New directions for the sociology of education*. London: Collier-Macmillan.

Young, R. (1990). *White mythologies: Writing, history and the West*. New York: Routledge.

Young, R. (1995). *Colonial desire: Hybridity in theory, culture and race*. London: Routledge.

INDEX